The Dirty Tricks of Negotiating

THE
DIRTY
TRICKS

OF   DISCOVER AND
       MASTER THE
       RULES OF NEGOTIATION

NEGOTIATING

George van Houtem

'While one stops to negotiate with a hawk,
nobody would think twice about devouring a dove'

Published by Haystack Publishing

P.O. Box 308
5301 BT Zaltbommel
The Netherlands

www.haystack.nl/thedirtytricksofnegotiating
needle@haystack.nl

Original title: De dirty tricks van het onderhandelen
Translation: Benjamin Roberts
Editing supervisor: Bram Gerrits
Book cover design: Foxy Design

ISBN: 9789461261519
NUR: 806, 800

CONTENTS

CHAPTER 2: THE OPENING PHASE 38

CHAPTER 3: THE DISCUSSION PHASE 52

CHAPTER 4: THE EXPLORATION PHASE 84

INTRODUCTION

Y ou negotiate more often than you think. Whether you are a businessman, politician, musician or marketing manager, you probably negotiate every day without realizing it. We negotiate every time we have a conversation and opinions differ, positions diverge or interests are in conflict. We negotiate every time we need the other party to make a decision.

We notice this every time there is a meeting and discussion. Whenever we have opposing opinions with other people and need to come to an agreement, negotiation kicks in.

We are negotiating more and more but that does not necessarily mean that everyone can pull it off easily or properly. Negotiation is one of the most difficult skills there is.

For one, it requires being committed to the goals you want to achieve. This calls for resolute behavior, which means acting confident, making clear demands or proposals, setting boundaries, and having nerves of steel.

Moreover, both parties need each other. Both are dependent on each other to reach an agreement. This requires paying attention to the relationship with the other party and showing a degree of sensitivity and understanding to their needs and interests.

At the same time you have to closely monitor the actual content of the topics being discussed. For example, is all the relevant knowledge available, is there anything missing, are the facts and figures correct, are the proposals in the proceedings practically feasable? What are the consequences of this outcome? This requires a rational approach: analyzing, being objective, taking time for deliberation, and exploring alternatives.

For the negotiator, the demands are almost impossible. He has to juggle: he has an assignment or an objective, while at the same time he also needs to cooperate, and keep a level head. This is often so difficult that many negotiators only focus on their own position. That's understandable, but it's also dangerous: for an optimal result the negotiator needs to focus on the counterparty as well.

The successful negotiator continuously takes into account the interests of the counterparty. What's his approach? What are the written and unwritten rules that are being applied?

What kind of people are on the other side of the table? Do they take into account the relationship between both parties or are they only interested in what's in it for them? Do they interact or do they keep a distance? Do they act as equals or do they try to dominate the talks? Does it feel like there is a degree of mutual openness and willingness to reach a goal? Or does distrust prevail, and are they playing games and using tricks?

As if the negotiator doesn't have enough to keep tabs on, he also has to take into account the needs of the party he represents. Are their demands reasonable? The negotiator constantly needs to verify whether he has full support of his own party when negotiating a deal.

Fortunately, in the last few decades many strategies have

been developed for negotiators. The following will be valuable to anyone who has to negotiate. They complement each other and can be used simultaneously.

DO'S AND DON'TS

For most negotiators, these are the basic rules of thumb for negotiation. The negotiation process can best be described as applying basic rules and tactical moves. By using these do's and don'ts, a negotiator will be successful:

- Think more about interests than specific targets.
- Allow plenty of time for exchanging information.
- Negotiate multiple issues simultaneously.
- Ask for more than you expect to get.
- Never accept the first offer.
- Take initiative.
- Be tough on content, soft on relationship.
- Taking the interests of the other party into account is not a sign of weakness.
- Explore alternatives.
- Don't turn negotiation into a debating event.
- Making concessions is part of the game.
- Wait as long as possible before making a concession.
- Ask for something in return for a concession.
- Don't be afraid to suspend a negotiation.
- Deadlocks are part of negotiating.
- Meet informally outside the meeting room.

THE PROCESS APPROACH

In this approach, the negotiation is presented as a process with several phases. Each phase has its own dynamics and rules, and requires different behavior from the negotiator. If the negotiator doesn't know these phases and their rules, it can go disastrously wrong.

A sales employee of an event agency negotiates with the manager of a conference center on the price of promotional stands, the number of square feet, catering, promotional activities and deadline for cancellation. Their initial proposals are far apart. The assertive sales employee is not up for a long discussion and offers what he considers to be a reasonable proposition: "Let's cut to the chase, we both know how this works and where it's going. Let's meet in the middle? Do we have a deal?"

To his surprise, the manager responds in a less cooperative manner. "I'm glad you're up for making concessions, because that's a luxury I can't afford. I can't meet in the middle."

The sales employee is taken back. What now? He's already handed over all his bargaining chips.

The salesperson was naive and too eager to cut a deal. He went from the opening phase - with a first exchange of positions - and jumped directly to offering a deal. That's going to cost him considerably.

Negotiations need time and have the following phases:

- *Preparation*: internal and external inventory, determine interests, objectives and strategy;
- *Opening*: formulating positions, interests, visions, principles, and objectives;
- *Discussion*: discussing arguments, getting to know what the other party really wants, determine priorities;
- *Exploring proposals*: entertaining alternatives;
- *Bargaining*: giving concessions back and forth;
- *Deadlock*: stalemate is part of negotiation;
- *Compromise*: building bridges to settle the final points, adding pressure and closing the deal.

PRINCIPLED NEGOTIATION

One of the world's most renowned methods of negotiation is called principled negotiation. It was designed by R. Fisher, W. Ury, and B. Patton of the Harvard Negotiation Project. This method presupposes that the negotiator must foremost be reasonable, and has to abide by a number of principles in order to be the most effective.

Two members of a local little league discuss remodeling the clubhouse. The president wants the clubhouse to be enlarged considerably, while the treasurer only wants it to be slightly modernized and to have a larger patio. What started as a friendly discussion gradually turns into a heated debate in which neither party is willing to give an inch. "I want a fifty foot extension to the backside leading out to the patio. I also think there should be a barbeque facility as well." The president adds, "The plastic doors and window frames also need to be replaced with wooden ones."

The treasurer replies irritated: "Absolutely not. Do you have any idea how much they cost? And that barbecue is definitely not going to happen. People hardly ever use the barbeque, and then it has to meet the safety requirements by the fire department."

The president is annoyed by the treasurer's remarks and takes it personally. He replies: "Your thinking is short-sighted. You are only thinking from the perspective of treasurer. We need people on the board who can think for the whole of the association."

Now the treasurer is really upset: "What are you saying, I'm not professional? If we follow your lead, the association will go bankrupt. If there is anyone thinking about interests of the association, then it's me!"

Now the president in turn is really upset. He retorts: "I won't let the future of the little league association be dictated by a two-bit accountant. That extension and barbecue pit is coming, hell or high water!" The treasurer pushes back his chair and stands up. He yells back: "You might be able to get your way as director of your company, but in our association we decide important matters like this democratically."

What started as a discussion about substance turned into an emotionally charged conflict. How can the board members of the local little league get out of this mess? Both have taken positions, exchanged insults, and are now angry at each other. This situation can be rescued with principled negotiation.

Separate people from problems

People have emotions. And certainly during negotiations, emotions can get the upper hand. Negotiators can get emotionally involved and experience the arguments of the other party as personal attacks. Negotiators will then fight each other instead of working on the problem that needs to be solved. In these situations, negotiators need to redirect their focus on substance. Smart negotiators address the problem working shoulder to shoulder, instead of back to back. In doing so, negotiators create a productive environment for negotiation.

Negotiate interests, not positions

Many negotiators pay close attention to standpoints and requirements. It is wiser, however, to focus on the interests and motives that lie behind the positions. By asking the *how* and *why* questions behind demands and requirements, negotiators will find out what the real needs and desires of the other party are. This will increase the number of possible solutions. Usually there are several possibilities to serve someone's interests and desires than the specific proposal that someone has put on the table.

Think of possibilities and solutions

As negotiator, don't look for solutions right away. Take time to explore the various possibilities with the other party.

This way negotiators let the other party know that they are not only interested in their own position but also in those of the other party. Separate creating possibilities from selecting solutions.

Use objective criteria to get to a decision

Don't let the decision be influenced by pressure, manipulation, or subjective judgment. Base it on objective criteria. Objective criteria should be reasonable and independent of the desires of both parties. Objective criteria are rational, based on procedures, legislation, market value, comparable situations, equality, reciprocity, percentage criteria, industry standards, scientific judgment, mathematical criteria, and precedents.

The president realizes that after a stalemate, negotiations have been suspended for too long. He needs to reopen the discussion. He doesn't want to make the same mistake and decides to use principled negotiation techniques. Now they have cooled down, it's time for them to return to the negotiation table.

The president resumes talks: "We're not getting any further this way, but you and I both want what's best for our club. We just think differently about getting there. I see that we both have the best interests of the club at heart. Our differences should not get in the way of reaching a good solution."

The president acknowledges the treasurer's good intentions and creates the right mood to resume discussions.

"I understand that you are against extending the building. Can you tell me why? Because I want to know your reasoning behind it."

The chairman does not argue with the opposing position of the treasurer. He wants to know his interests or motives behind his standpoint. By asking, they might find common ground.

The concerned treasurer says: "I'm worried about the costs of the remodeling will bring. Will we still be able to pay for two new trainers?" He adds, "In our current financial situation, we can just barely get by."

The president responds: "I see our league grow significantly within the next five years. With the housing development in the neighborhood with many young families, I don't want a run-down little league clubhouse. It should be a place where people can comfortably sit and enjoy themselves."

The president doesn't immediately suggest a new proposal but first wants to find out what the costs for both options will include.

"Let's first explore our options. We'll write the different proposals on a flipchart. Lets define the criteria that our proposal has to meet. What are important criteria for you?"

"I think that the interest should not increase our budget. With the additional interest costs, we have to increase our turnover." The president agrees and then adds his own criteria: "I think our clubhouse should be up to standards with other clubhouses."

Throughout the rest of the talks, the two men have determined both criteria to be an important basis for reaching a possible solution. With this approach, both members of the board of the little league association have made it less personal. They now know each other's motives and interests, and can jointly opt for a solution that takes both parties' interests into account because they have recognized each other's interests together.

THE DILEMMA APPROACH

According to the negotiation theory of Willem Masterbroek, Dutch professor emiritus of Organizational Culture and Communication, there are four activities involved in negotiation that are directly related to four basic dilemmas:

Substance: how tough or soft am I going to be in reaching my goals and requirements?

You are at the negotiation table to achieve results. It usually involves interests, objectives, policies, standards, and proposals. How firm are you going to be in order to achieve them? Are you taking a tough position or opting for a soft approach?

Power: how tough or soft are you going to act during the negotiations?

If you want your opponent to take you seriously, then the power difference should not be too great. Both parties should realize that they need each other. Yet, most likely the other will try to test your strength. Do not let the other party take advantage of you, and ensure that the other party doesn't have an edge on you. This will immediately instigate fighting behavior from the other side, which will not improve the negotiations.

Approach: how willing, jovial, distant, hostile should I act?

Negotiation benefits from a certain degree of cooperative behavior. Respect and understanding for the other party and their interests contribute to a good negotiating environment. A hostile approach will result in distrust and irritation, and can impede negotiations significantly.

Procedure: how active and interested in the other party do I want to come across during the negotiation? Or should I act more passive and laidback?

Increasing procedural flexibility adds to the boundaries of negotiation. However, this requires that the negotiator be assertive and interested in gathering information. He has to be flexible when inquiring about the other parties underlying interests and motives, and asking many questions. He has to put a real effort in finding alternative solutions. When a negotiator is cautious, it may comes across as disinterest, especially when he is not concerned about the other party, or willing to explore different options.

The inexperienced negotiator cannot differentiate between the four activities. He either applies the tough, top dog approach or the soft one. He combines championing his goals with dominant behavior, and repeats his arguments. Or he drops his demands because he wants to keep the mood at the negotiation table pleasant. A negotiator is more effective when he can differentiate between the four activities. By detaching himself from his own pursuits and maintaining a friendly atmosphere at the negotiation table, he can explore other options.

THE DIRTY TRICKS OF NEGOTIATING

Being reciprocal and finding common interests is key in all negotiation. A negotiator should always strive for a win-win situation. This is a noble cause but in practice it sometimes falls to the wayside because the other party pursues only his own interests. While the negotiator follows a proven strategy, the other party uses a dirty trick.

This is not a theoretical book with a recipe for winning every negotiation. This is a pragmatic book, in which the reader will find out the *do's* and *don'ts* of negotiation. In my practice as a professional negotiator and adviser to negotiators my experience is that you must stick to the rules, but also be aware of the unwritten ones. In this book I will discuss both the written and the unwritten rules, the dirty tricks, so the reader will know which pitfalls to avoid when negotiating with someone who has a hidden agenda. This book will help the reader recognize the most common dirty tricks so that they can be properly dealt with.

Are you up for negotiations in which you collaborate to achieve a goal that is beneficial to both parties? First, make sure you know what a dirty trick looks like before you get left holding the empty bag.

1

THE PREPARATION PHASE

Preparation separates a good negotiator from a bad one. An inexperienced negotiator spends less time preparing than an experienced one. In any negotiation, good prep work is half the battle. If you still have to gather information during negotiations, then you stand to be seriously behind in the game.

During negotiations, there will be a lot of information and emotions for you to process. Your attention and energy should not be focused on issues you could have prepared in advance. You should concentrate on what has been put on the table, and not be distracted by lack of knowledge, or have doubts about the scope of the negotiation. From the start, those matters should already be clear. During the preparation phase, you'll set the stage of the negotiations. That will give you an important edge throughout the talks.

DETERMINING INTERESTS AND GOALS

During the preparatory phase, you analyze the situation, determine all possible options, and above all, set your goals and strategies. Many negotiators focus on specific demands and draft elaborate proposals. A lot of emphasis is put on claims that support their position. Certainly, these aspects are important, but they only come in handy during a later stage in the game.

The first thing you need to do is make sure you are clear about the interests hidden behind the proposal you initially drafted. This will give you a clearer view of what your concerns and objectives really are. Moreover, it will increase the bargaining leeway during negotiations. There are several ways to determine where your interests lie and how you can achieve your objectives.

An executive secretary prepares for her annual review with her supervisor. She wants a raise. She comes up with a concrete proposal and considers the various points they will discuss. Eventually, she has the courage to say: "Given the nature of my job and the hours I make, I'd like a five percent raise."

"I completely understand where you're coming from," her supervisor replies sympathetically. "If anyone deserves a raise, it's you. Unfortunately, no raises or bonuses can be given this year. We are having to significantly cut back our budget."

"Oh, I had no idea. What a shame. Never mind, then."

The two then lapse into a bout of small talk before ending the conversation. As the executive secretary walks to the door, she says to her boss: "That's really a shame about the raise. I was hoping to go to night school and get a bachelors degree in psychology. Guess it'll have to wait until next year."

"Wait," her boss says. "What was that you said? Something about paying for a degree? We can certainly help you out there. Those kinds of expenses fall under training costs. We get a grant for that. That's no problem at all."

The executive secretary was fortunate that she was ultimately able to give her reason for wanting a raise in the first place. That gave her manager the opportunity to help her achieve her objective – the ability to complete her degree in psychology. He was unable to accommodate her original (and only) request of a five percent raise. However, he was able to help her with what she really wanted.

Once your interests are clear, you can translate them into concrete proposals. Do not focus all of your energy on the precise formulation of the proposal or its solution. If you put those blinders on, you won't be able to see the other possible solutions that can result from negotiations. If that happens, you risk negotiations getting bogged down early in the game.

Instead, do everything you can to give yourself room to manoeuvre. To avoid fighting tooth and nail defending just one proposal, try developing multiple proposals or several variations on one proposal as part of your preparation. There is more than one road that leads to Rome. This gives you more leeway at the negotiating table. Take the time to come up with alternatives in advance. What are your goals and what are the ways you can achieve them? Stay open to options and suggestions. Don't get stuck on just one specific outcome.

KNOW YOUR BOTTOM PRICE

Negotiation based on interests does not mean there are no priorities or boundaries. They absolutely exist. However, many negotiators neglect to clearly define what they wish to achieve. They might be vague on which outcome will satisfy them or when to turn down an offer.

A cooperative of GP's in Chicago consists of 40 physicians with *single and group practices. The doctors in the cooperative jointly decide to integrate diabetes care. After talks, a well-known health insurance company offers $1,050 annually per patient for diabetic care from the cooperative. The cooperative accepts the insurer's proposition.*

The physicians all agree it's an adequate amount. They calculate they should easily earn $150 per diabetic when all is said and done.

The cooperative of GP's then contract various health care providers, including an optomitrist, a physical therapist, and a nutritionist. The optomitrist wants $50 per consultation, the laboratory costs $80, and the nutritionist wants $50 per diabetic patient in exchange for her services. Finally, the physical therapist charges $70 per patient. That brings the cooperative's total costs to $750,000.

After everyone has taken their cut, the cooperative figures out they stand only to earn $300,000. The doctors ask themselves,"how did that happen?" The answer is painfully simple: bad prep work. Beforehand, the cooperative should have figured out the cost per diabetic.This would have prevented them from negotiating for such a small margin between insurer and the various health care providers.

The cooperative is only making $100 instead of $150 on each diabetic patient. "This isn't worth it", the disappointed doctors complain. "We can't run the practice on that."

Every negotiator should know what their bottom price is. If you don't have one, there is a good chance you'll repeatedly drop your price. You are likely to get swept away by the heat of negotiating and before you know it, you will accept an offer you would have never have agreed to beforehand. In advance, avoid having post-negotiation regret by setting your bottom offer. Determine your lowest offer before you start.

KNOW YOUR OPPOSITION

The players at the negotiating table will largely determine the negotiation process. Therefore, it is a good idea to not only know your topics in advance but also know the people with whom you'll be negotiating.

What kind of negotiating partners are you up against? Dominant or rational? Are they focused more on getting their interests pushed through or are they out to please everyone? Experienced or inexperienced? Are they "one-man shows" or do they rely on their backers when they have to make decisions? These are questions you need to ask.

Too often, the negotiator focuses only on the content and neglects taking the personalities he will be negotiating with into account. During the meetings you'ill be dealing directly with the other negotiator. You'll need to deal with his personality and behavior.

If you are more a rational and cooperative type and the opposing negotiator is a dominant, pitbull type of guy, it's probably a good idea to have a more assertive colleague do the negotiating. Is it really wise for you - a results-driven negotiator – to be put in a negotiation with an uncertain buyer, who wants security? Or should your patient, more analytical colleague lead the talks?

Ask colleagues about their experience and if they have

any tips. Unfortunately, a cunning negotiator on the other side of the table will often pull all the tricks out of his hat every time he negotiates. This works because each time he is dealing with a different negotiator who hasn't bothered to do his homework.

Address the possible concerns, wishes, and objectives of the other person. What is the outcome he needs to bring back home, and what are the expectations from the people he is representing? Where do they stand? Consult their annual report and search Google for info about the company and the negotiators you'll be dealing with.

Who will be sitting in front of you? Will you be going into negotiations alone, or will someone else be accompanying you? And if so, who will that be? Do you have the same type of personality or are you complete opposites? People often find working with individuals who are more or less the same in terms of attitude and behavior to be more enjoyable. You connect better and feel more at ease with them.

However, you'll probably be a stronger negotiating team if you and your colleague are completely different. A competitive negotiator together with a more rationally-minded colleague makes for a better combo than two competitive types. And a rational, analytical negotiator partnered with a relational-oriented coworker is more effective than two analytical types. When putting together your negotiating team, make sure to have a good mix of people who are consistent, are analytical, and people-skills, as well as those with expertise and experience.

INFLUENCING YOUR BACKERS

Going to the negotiation table with a mission for getting high objectives and only armed with restricted authority will limit your flexibility. You won't be very effective. Creating bargaining leeway starts with the preliminary meetings with your backers. They expect you to get the most out of the negotiation. Afterall, that's why they hired you. They will make demands that might be unrealistic.

If you are not careful, you will find yourself caught between two parties with very different expectations: your backers on the one side, and the negotiator from the other party on the other. Both parties want something from you, but their wishes are completely opposite from each other.

You can avoid being put in an impossible situation beforehand by tempering expectations. Urge your backers to consider multiple alternatives, and not just one. Do not exclude possibilities. Ask your backers to prioritize their interests and indicate their objectives. Then you know where you can be flexible, and where you need to stand firm.

Make sure you have sufficient mandate. If your backers give you unlimited mandate, you run the risk of disappointing them. "This isn't what we had expected," they'll say. If your backers are completely unsatisfied, you will likely be sent back to the negotiation table, which is not desirable. This adds tension to the relationship you have with the other party, as well the relationship you have with your backers. Your credibility with both of them will suffer. On the other hand, a mandate that is too limited can be paralyzing. You will not have enough leeway to explore and haggle.

Do not wait for your backers to give you authority. *Tell them* how much mandate you need to get the job done.

The following checklist will ensure that you don't overlook anything and will be able to take advantage of every opportunity.

PREP CHECKLIST

Content

- Who has expertise or experience with this topic?
- Are we sufficiently familiar with the dossier we've put together? Do we know enough about the topic for negotiation? Do we need additional information?
- Is our dossier complete? Are we missing anything?
- What are our interests and goals?
- What are our priorities?
- What are the interests and goals of the other party?
- What is, for us:
  - an ideal outcome,
  - a realistic outcome
  - an unacceptable outcome?
- What are their expected highest and lowest objectives?
- How do we open? What is our highest defensible bid?
- What arguments will we use?
- What are our concessions?

- Which order will we present them? What will we ask in return for a certain concession?
- What negotiation procedure do we want to follow?
- What criteria or principles do we want to follow?

Relational

- What is the background of the other party and its negotiators?
- What type of negotiators are we up against?
- Is our team complementary enough? What does that look like?
- What is the expected mood at the negotiating table?
- Do we need the other party to do what we want? Are they important for us in the future?
- Who has the upper hand? What does that look like?
- Where are we dependent on each other? Do we have any shared interests?
- What alternatives or options do they have at their disposal?
- What are the consequences for both sides if they don't come to an agreement?
- What kind of tricks can we expect?
- How important is the headquarters during the negotiations?
- What are the time constraints (for us, and for them)?
- Where will the negotiations take place?

THE BAIT

Everyday we are overwhelmed with ad slogans such as "Fly to London for just $750." Or, "LCD-screens for $175." Or, "Volkswagen Golf now available as low as $18,000."

Websites and stores constantly lure us with special offers. However, once they reel you in, you discover that the offer is no longer available. Instead of walking out the door, many people stick around to see if there might be another interesting offer. It is very likely that a sale will be made, though this new offer will often be less attractive than the one the customers originally came to the (online) store for.

The customers have been duped. Had they known beforehand they would be paying a higher price, they never would have gone into the store in the first place. However, the offer stimulated their desire to buy. It was so strong that, once inside, the buyers concocted all kinds of excuses to justify the more expensive purchase, despite that it was of no real benefit to them.

"Eight hundred and sixty dollars isn't a bad deal. A round-trip, non-stop flight to Seattle costs almost as much."

"You know, our television is old, we need to replace it soon anyway. Since we're here, we might as well go ahead and buy this one for $299."

This same bait is also used in negotiation.

Two companies merge to create a new company. The new board of directors wants to throw a party for the employees to celebrate the merger. They thought it would be a good way to encourage a sense of company unity.

A project leader was asked to negotiate with a large event planning company. The company suggests hosting the party at Disneyland Resorts. According to them, two new attractions will be opening around the time the party will take place. Employees can check out the new attractions without having to stand in line. But the project leader has her doubts. California is a bit far, after all. However, the whole affair just fits in the budget allocated for the event. She thinks there must surely be more original and less expensive options that are closer to home.

"Oh", says the representative from the event planning company. "I forgot to mention that Bruce Springsteen will also be giving an exclusive concert at Disneyland. Your employees will get front row seats."

"This is a once-in-a-lifetime chance", the project leader thinks to herself. "I can't pass this up". She decides to take up the offer from the event planning company.

The office building is buzzing with excitement about the party's location and Bruce Springsteen. A month before the party, the project leader gets a call from the event planning company.

"I'm sorry to disappoint you, but my colleague was mistaken. The Bruce Springsteen concert has been canceled. But there will be a performance by the Irish step dancing spectacle Riverdance. As compensation, we can offer you a room upgrade at the hotel."

The project leader is fed up. If she had known this earlier, she would have never agreed to the Disneyland offer. Under these new conditions, the location does not sound that great any more. But by *now, the entire company is excited. Canceling the event is no longer an option. So she takes the upgrade.*

This principle is no different than the bait used in ads. The negotiator was reeled in under false pretenses. The original teaser is withdrawn before the deal is finalized and when it is far more difficult to say no. The negotiator is faced with a dilemma. Backing out is too much of a hassle but the new offer is not as attractive as the first one that was promised. Had it been made clear in advance, the negotiator would never have agreed in the first place.

What do you do in a case like this? Set your limits and conditions during preparation. Share these with others on your team. You really have to defend yourself when this dirty trick is used. In so doing, you avoid falling into the trap of looking for excuses to justify continuing discussions or accepting new conditions when the initial, more attractive offer from the other party falls through. Others can point this out to you, saving you from having to rationalize it.

Make it difficult for the other party to withdraw a specific offer. Be clear up front as to what the consequences will be if the other party fails to comply with their original offer. One example is the termination of negotiations with a predetermined compensation. Do not be afraid to demand ample settlement. Be wary if the other party is unwilling to commit. Could it be that they already know they won't be able to live up to his promises?

DIRTY TRICK
SCARE TACTICS

Negotiators are often forced into making quick decisions about a proposal. You'll hear things like: others are also interested, prices are going up next week, this will no longer be allowed under the upcoming legislation, the economy is weakening, and so is the demand for your product.

Let's face it: you'll be lucky to make a deal at all under these circumstances. However, the question is how real are each of these scares. The purpose of this dirty trick is to make sure the negotiator isn't well prepared. He is likely to accept the proposal without consulting anybody or doing any research.

These threats might scare you and prevent you from preparing yourself sufficiently. You might not have enough time to consider all the alternatives for and the consequences of the offer that has been proposed. In any case, the negotiator's perception has been altered. This dirty trick changes his grasp on the situation, and his position at the negotiation table has been weakened.

What do you do in this situation? Keep your responses neutral and ask for arguments. Where is this threat coming from? Consider if you would still accept the deal if the threat did not exist. If that is not the case, offer your regrets and tell them you need more time to think before making a decision. Or let them know that you cannot accept the offer under threats. Act like their scares have no influence on you. Stay calm, cool, and collected.

2

THE OPENING
PHAS
E

Finally you are sitting across from the other party, and the negotiation is about to begin. The opening is very important. Here you lay the groundwork for how the negotiation will unfold. During this phase, you'll get a good idea about each other's desires and motives. You'll size up your own position and that of the other party. You'll assess what is feasible for both sides. Therefore it's important to understand the other party's take on the situation. That way you can influence the situation in your favor. This starts immediately from the beginning. Both parties want to know what to expect, and how the other one is going to approach the talks. How will these negotiations proceed and what is the procedure going to be? But most importantly, what are the chances that you are going to get what you want.

Sticking to the following tactics makes a good start.

SIZE UP YOUR CHANCES

Start the negotiation by asking everyone to introduce themselves. After that, pass out an agenda for the talks, the way you would like the negotiaton to proceed. Ask the other party if they agree with your proposal. Check how much of a mandate the other negotiator has. Can he make decisions on his own? Or does he first have to confirm with others? After that, allow the other party first to lay out their wishes and interests. Ask questions about their requests. Make sure that you clearly understand the rationale and motives behind their objectives. What are the priorities and which principles are the most important?

Hold off going into discussion. Let the other side finish. During this stage it is especially important that it becomes clear what is important for the other party, and that you create the right mood for the negotiations. The opening phase is likely to feel awkward for the negotiators at times.

Four team leaders at an insurance company discuss how the new flexible workspaces will be divided up among the teams. The teamleader of the department of homeowner's insurance explains why he is entitled to have all those workspaces: "Considering the increase in the number of FTEs on my team, I need the space for my staff."

"Excuse me!" replies the teamleader from life insurance. "They are flexible workplaces, you can't claim them for yourself. You know what? I'll take all the spots near the window."

"You've got no right to fixed locations because you've got primarily part-timers on your team," responds the team leader from mortgages.

"I want at least 12 fixed locations, the other workspaces can be shared," claims the team leader from car insurance. "I think you shouldn't be entitled to no more than six fixed workspaces, your team has been reduced in FTE's."

Before the team leaders know each other's needs and interests, their explanations have been vented, and the discussion is already at a deadlock.

However tempting it might be to respond to what the other party says, it is wiser to wait and let them finish with their viewpoints before expressing yours. Make a list of all the expectations and assumptions. Make sure you get all the information. After the other party has expressed their desires and wishes, you can explain your interests and expectations. During this stage, avoid directly discussing proposals and demands. It is highly probable that conflicting viewpoints will prevail. During this phase it is important to find common interests and assumptions. How this can be used in the negotiation process will be discussed shortly.

THE IDEAL FIRST MOVE

After making an inventory of each other's desires and assumptions, the moment arrives when you and the other party must come up with concrete proposals. The first move is important. It determines your starting position and your flexibility during the rest of the negotiation proceedings. It also affects the other party's perception about the feasibility of its objectives.

Negotiators that expect to achieve their goals are more likely to get their objectives than those whose expectations have been tempered from the start. That is why it is important from the start to play down their expectations. If this happens the other way around, the other party will provoke you. If you know what will instigate the first response from the other party, you can influence and manoeuvre your own expectations and behaviors, and consequently those of the other party as well.

First, make the opening bid

By putting your bid out first, you set a psychological anchor for the other party. Few people are immune to the psychological power of the first stake in the ground. They will have to adapt their counterproposal to your opening bid. It also works the other way around. If they make the first offer, you have to adapt your proposal to their bid.

A tax expert negotiates an assignment in the final phase. It is a review of a subsidiary: a half-day of preparation, six sessions of interviews, two sessions a day required to write reports, and then present the findings.

The remuneration of the work is discussed. The director of the subsidiary requests an estimate of the allocated cost considering the budget is limited and there are bids from other firms. The tax expert contemplates: should he take the initiative and give the actual costs, or should he first ask what the budget is?

He decides not to give an estimate, but asks for the budget. The director smiles and responds: "Our budget is limited to $5,500." The tax expert feels uneasy. His normal rate is $800 a session, but an offer of $8,000 for a day would exceed the other party's budget. He decides to lower his offer to $6,000 a day.

By leaving the initiative to the other party, the tax expert got caught holding the short end of the stick. When the discrepancy between the opening bid and yours is too great, then you have to adjust yours towards their initial offer. Consequently, you have just made the first concession, without them knowing it. This mistake can be easily avoided by taking the first initiative.

Make an offer that is the most justifiable

Of course, in most cases, the final outcome will deviate from your original opening bid. Concessions are part of the game. Where you end up, usually depends on the content of your first proposal. It all depends on how much or how little you offer in terms of price, volume, and margin. Which requirements or conditions are you asking for? The more assertive you are willing to be during the negotiation, the more leeway you will have for the rest of the negotiation talks.

Negotiators are often scared of taking a chance. Some think "they will never accept this" and consequently start with a lower offer than one that would have been justifiable. Some negotiators even head directly for a compromise. Never, *ever*, do that!

If you start with an offer that has been less than what you really want, then you end up *compromising* on a *compromise*. The worse thing is that the other party won't even know that you bargained yourself down. He doesn't even know that your starting bid had been marked down, and is likely to ask you again, later during the negotiations to make more concessions. If you do not have much bargaining room left, the other party is likely to consider you unreasonable and unwilling. If you easily agree to the other party's demands, you are likely to comprimise your own needs and objectives.

Do not make a compromise. But do not ask for the grand

prize either. Your proposal has to be justifiable. What is your proposal based on; which arguments, facts, legislation, precedents support your offer? If you cannot defend your proposal, then you are probably asking too much. Although the urge to bluff or lie might be hard to surpress, don't let yourself be tempted. A professional opposing party will always question and ask for evidence supporting your offer, if they have any doubt. Trust is essential, so maintain a good relationship during negotiations.

Present your objectives in the form of a proposal

Some negotiators put an entire proposal, bid or requirement on the table. They will ask the other party for a detailed package. This is a definite no, no because it is a lot harder for the other party to accept a complete proposal, whether in the form of an offer or a demand.

Never accept the first proposal from the other party

In situations where the other party makes the first offer, it is smarter to turn it down even if it meets your needs, or if it is better than the outcome you had initially hoped for. As strange as it might sound, turning down the first offer is also good for the other party. By accepting their opening bid, you'll immediately get one of two responses: the other party will think he has underpriced himself, or there is a catch. Instead of feeling good about the deal, he will either feel disappointed or distrust you.

And the next time the other party will try to get more out of you and raise the stakes.

During the preliminary talks between representatives of a project and the chairman of the school board about the budget and the timeframe they state: "For developing a new teaching methodology and implementing the new educational system, we need $60,000 and 12 disposable hours." The chairman of the school board replies, "Okay, that's acceptable."

While it seems like the deal is sealed, the representatives walk away dissatisfied and wonder if they should have asked for more money and demanded more man hours. Were their calculations correct, had they overlooked something?

DIRTY TRICK
THE AUCTION

This dirty trick is often used by buyers and procurement representatives. During the first round of negotiations, the procuring party will give you - the vendor - the chance to make a salespitch about the advantages and favorable conditions he has to offer. What you don't know is that the procuring party is also doing it with several other suppliers.

During the second round, he confronts you with a similar or even better offer from other vendors. Any additional conditions and requirements demanded by the competing suppliers are obviously not mentioned. Suddenly your offer from the first round does not seem good enough. What can you offer to get the deal?

Because you do not want to lose out, you might feel the urge to make the deal sweeter by offering even better conditions or benefits. Through the tactic of the auction, you'll be tricked into giving all your information away and you'll be played out against other bidders.

To put the pressure on, the other party might even let you see the competition. You'll "accidently" run into them in the hallway or there will be a memo on the negotiaton table with another vendor's name on it. What do you do in this case?

Ask the other party to be open about the conditions

Instead of telling all the benefits of your offer during the first negotiation round, ask the other party which conditions they want included in the contract. Ask them what their priorities and deeper interests are. Then it is up to you to determine whether you can meet those conditions. If it is possible, you can tell them that you are willing to meet them, somewhere in the middle, provided that the terms are unconditional, and included in the agreement. You run the risk that the other party is asking too much, but that is alright because you are still negotiating. This way you won't be played out during the second round.

Stick to your guns

Do not get caught up in the frenzy of the auction. Instead of getting drawn into the comparisons with other suppliers, stick to the conditions of your initial offer. Do not try to match the combinated proposals from other bidding parties. Change the scope of the negotiations and come up with new concessions and alternatives in other areas. This way you prevent being compared with other competiting parties.

Keep to a minimum

Never forget what your bottom price is. Question - at all times - if the demanded conditions are beneficial to your objectives. However tempting it might be to want to strike a deal, sometimes during a negotiation it will gradually seem like none of the conditions are beneficial to you.

DIRTY TRICK
EXTREME PROPOSAL

Sometimes parties throw an extreme proposal on the table that they know is not realistic. Consequently, they want you to get the idea that you have miscalculated the situation. All of a sudden, your proposal and desired objectives seem unrealistic. This way they will try to get you to lower your expectations. You can protect yourself from this trick by not coming up with a counteroffer. Instead ask the the other party to come up with a more a realistic proposal.

By giving pertinent facts, financial or legal issues, you show them that you know what a realistic proposal is. You can put pressure on the negotiation by telling the person what the consequences of his actions are. For example, say: "I don't think this is a constructive way to start negotiating." Or, "This way, I don't have much faith that we're going to get anywhere." Or, "If you don't come up with another proposal, you leave me no choice except to come up with an extreme counterproposal. Is that what you want?"

If you still want to continue, you can offer a counterproposal: "I think this is an outlandish proposal. I get the idea you're trying to trick me into lowering my proposal. This is not the way I want to negotiate. However, I assume this is not your intention. I'll give you the opportunity to come up with another opening bid."

DIRTY TRICK
FIRST BID IS FINAL OFFER

Sometimes it seems as if the offer is non-negotiable. You've been given an final offer, and you haven't even started negotiating. The person who uses this tactic, positions himself as a tough negotiator. He is not prepared to make concessions and not open to alternatives. At least, that is how he wants to come across. It is a risky approach because the talks have gotten serious, and there is not much room for discussion. During negotiations people want to exert their influence, and the end result should be determined by their negotiating skills. By putting the "first bid *and* final offer" on the table, it ruins the chances of the talks ever reaching an agreement. At the beginning of a negotiation, many negotiators will perceive "a first bid as final offer" as a loss of face. Therefore they are likely to turn it down, even though it is a good deal for them.

This dirty trick seems smart. Unfortunately, it's not. The negotiator that puts an offer like this on the table, gives up control over the talks. Now it is up to the other party to determine how the rest of the negotiation will play out. In this situation, you have a number of options. For one, you can just ignore it, and act as if you did not hear it and continue exploring alternative proposals. Two, you can change the scope of negotiation. You can add new components to the content, and thus include a variation to the original proposal on the table. Now, you can both start talking again. Three, you can also go for deadlock. By replying to the other party's offer with your final offer will put both of you at complete opposite ends of the spectrum. Now the other party has their back against the wall. He can either accept your offer, or start negotiating.

By the way, if the "final offer" is favorable, you can also just accept it, with or without losing face.

DIRTY TRICK
THE ULTIMATUM

When the other party makes an ultimatum, they are putting you under pressure. Setting a deadline forces a decision. A proposal with a deadline can be both reasonable and unreasonable.

A couple negotiates with the bank for a mortgage. "I can give you this mortgage at 5.4% interest for five years," says the mortgage consultant. "But this offer is only valid until next Friday. Depending on the current interest rate, I will have to adjust the quote."

In this example, the offer's duration can be rationally argumented. It is backed by a perfectly valid explanation. Fluctuating rates affect the interest rates at banks daily. The offer is based on a temporary fixed situation. Therefore, it is understandable why the bank can only offer it for a limited period. The greater the external uncertainty factors are, the greater this risk is to the bank that can offer a specific interest rate deal on a mortgage.

To her delight, an applicant finds out that she is offered a job that she applied for. When it comes to discussing the terms of the contract, she is told that she has to accept their offer by the end of the day."Otherwise, they will withraw their offer," says the HR manager.

Now it's a different story. The ultimatum is used to put her under pressure and make her decide quickly. The HR manager wants to prevent the applicant from asking for additional demands, or possibly accepting another job offer. Time and having more options gives the applicant more bargaining power. Giving an ultimatum prevents and reduces that.

You'll almost never know for sure when a deadline is a hard deadline. Ask yourself what you think about the content of the proposal. Is it acceptable? Do you have any doubts? Would you accept it without a deadline?

In the latter case, you can let them know that you unfortunately cannot accept their offer under those conditions and would like more time to discuss the terms. In this kind of situation, you can also add your own terms. "If you force me to decide now, then unfortunately I cannot offer more than this. I would like to consider variables that are probably better for you and myself. But your ultimatum doesn't allow for that." The other party is now confronted with the negative consequences of their ultimatum. Now it's up to them to make a choice.

You can also accept the proposal under the condition they accept some of your demands. In any case, you are back discussing with the other party. They will respond to your request and for the moment, the ultimatum is off the table. Or you can also let the time limit expire, and just see what happens. Most likely the talks will ressume.

If you have doubts, then you can always ask to have the deadline extended. That way you win more time to make a decision. "I won't be able to give you an answer by then, but a day later, I can let you know what I have decided." Or, "my supervisor has to have a look at it and she won't be back by Tuesday. But Thursday she will be back and I can give you an answer by then." Or, "I will do my best to give you an answer by then. If I don't, then I can give you an answer early next week at the latest."

Try it anyway. If your efforts to extend the deadline fail, you can always accept the ultimatum.

3

THE DISCUSSI N PHASE

After presenting each other's opening proposals, it is time to swap arguments and test each other's tenacity and determination. A good negotiation requires tough discussion. You want your proposals and positions to come across as legitimate as possible, right? That's why it is important to get a good feeling for the other party and to know with whom you are dealing. During this phase, negotiation will seem like psychological warfare. And that is a good thing. It's the moment for each party to present themselves convincingly, and find out who's the weaker party.

THE DEBATE

During this phase it is important that you present strong arguments for your own position as well as provide well-argued replies to the arguments and questions from the other party. Here are some debating techniques that will help you increase your leverage.

Limit your number of arguments

Some negotiators will present numerous arguments, thinking that they are making their case stronger. Unfortunately, this only shows that the negotiator is inexperienced. Firing a barrage of arguments allows for the other party to pick apart more arguments and often comes across as being weak. Instead, present just a limited amount of strong arguments during the debate.

A trainee lawyer discusses a draft agreement with the lawyer from the other party. The agreement also contains several clauses which are detrimental to the other party. She knows that the other party won't accept these conditions that easily and will ask for some kind of justification.

She prepares herself well and examines which evidence can be used to support her arguments. After carefully weighing the arguments, she reduces it to five arguments: two are strong from a legal perspective, two are plausible, and one is somewhat questionable. Later, while discussing the draft agreement, the other party asks, as expected, for the legitimacy of the adverse clauses. At that point, she confidently gives her two strong arguments. Instead of responding and asking for substantial evidence, the laywer from the other party, asks the opposing lawyer if she had finished her plea, and if there is additional arguments to justify the adverse conditions. The lawyer trainee knows that the coast is clear to present her other arguments.

Then it's the experienced lawyer's turn. The entire time she has carefully listened and not responded to the strong arguments made by her colleague lawyer. Now, she carefully picks the weakest argument out and starts taking that one apart. The trainee lawyer becomes insecure. From all her arguments, the other lawyer is going after the argument that is the least convincing. But she is not going to take it sitting down and goes on the defense. However, for the trainee lawyer, the damage has already been done. The rest of the negotiation focuses only on her weakest argument. Her strong arguments are completely ignored. Her persuasiveness was ineffective. The trainee lawyer asks herself, "How could this have happened? Why couldn't I have convinced her, after all I had five arguments?"

Not in spite of, but *because* she had five arguments, it went all wrong. If another party is not already convinced after listening to two or three strong arguments, then chances are, they won't be convinced after hearing one more. Especially when the arguments presented later are usually the weaker ones. A barrage of arguments is more likely to put the other party off. This usually spoils the mood during the rest of the talks. You'll be more effective when you limit your arguments. Keep it to two or three reasons to support your case. When you get objections and persistent criticism from the other party, stop arguing your case and remark to the other party that there is a difference in opinion or perspective. Put the subject to the side and start discussing other topics.

Structure and categorize your arguments

People remember information when it is presented in a structure. Do not go directly for your most substantive argument right away. First categorize or prioritize it:

"From an organizational viewpoint, I suggest ..."
"As a legal argument I propose ..."
"The three main arguments are ..."
"The main reason I think ..."
"This is apparent according to following two studies ..."

"There are three different categories, the first of which ..."

"I will explain this with two examples ..."

Start and conclude with the strongest arguments

The first and last argument have the greatest impact. This is also called the primacy and the recency effect. The person on the other side of the negotiation table will always remember your first and last argument best. Present your strongest arguments at the beginning and at the end of your talk.

Use persuasive language

Not only does the content of your arguments count, but also the way you present it. Present your arguments with certainty. "This phrase evokes opposition and therefore I would like to have it removed from the statement" sounds different than "It might be a good idea to delete the phrase because it might cause opposition."

Inexperienced negotiators often use language that sounds doubtful. For example, they use diminutives and include nuances that are unnecessary. This weakens their persuasiveness. "If possible, I would like to propose a minor change in the terms" comes across as less certain than "Now , I want these changes made in the conditions."

Present arguments as absolute and definite

The more you present your arguments as "matter of fact", the sooner the other party will accept them to be true and definite:

"In similar situations, the following criteria are always used ..."
"From a just viewpoint, it should be obvious that the compensation is based on this allocation ..."

Presenting facts as absolute truths has the same effect. The other party will be less likely to question them:

"We don't have enough time to re-address this matter..."
"Despite what I think, the board will not even consider this option, so it is not worth discussing ..."

CONTROLING THE POWER GAME

To negotiate effectively, a certain balance of power is necessary. In practice there will almost always be one party that has a stronger position than the other. Your opponent may have other candidates to negotiate with than you. This power discrepancy may arise from differences in experience, knowledge, and skills between the negotiators. However, the difference should not be too great. To a certain extent the negotiators should have a feeling that they are dependent on each other. If the gap in power is too wide, then this will result in one party dominating the weaker one. It is important that power flows back and forth between both parties.

Grab the bull by the horns

During the talks you can strengthen your position by grabbing the reigns at the beginning. You can do this in several ways. For one, prior to the negotiation, you can determine the order of the items you want to discuss. For example, you can ask yourself if you want the most important item discussed at the beginning of the talks, when your mind is still sharp and there is plenty of time, or if you want to save it for the end, when the other party is tired and wants to go home.

You can also gain influence by trying to adjust the proceedings. You can alter the course of the negotiations by explicitly setting what the next stage will be. This is especially effective when negotiating with several parties. It can give a solid advantage. It makes a big difference whether a decision is by consensus or determined by majority vote.

A multinational company is negotiating with a major IT company about the design requirements of a new and expensive IT project. The project is stuck in the discussion phase. Both parties exchange arguments and concerns about necessity, feasibility and cost. The parties are at complete opposite ends and the mood is tense. The negotiator of the IT company tries to move past the stalemate and intervenes: "We keep repeating our differing viewpoints. Instead of trying to convince each other, let's focus on what we both agree on. I suggest we end the debate and try to forge a proposal. That way we will at least have a base from which we can proceed."

By calling for a transition from one phase to next, the negotiator moves the negotiation forward. Instead of being on opposing sides, they are now back together and can move forward and come up with a basic proposal on which all parties could agree. Obviously, both parties will still need to address the problem areas, but for the time being, they will have created a foundation that binds both of them. At that time, the need and the desire to work together is greater than in the discussion phase.

You can also take control by making substantive proposals. Then it is up to the other party to reply. They may either reject the proposal, make changes or at best accept it. If they turn the proposal down, you can come up with an alternative or ask them under what conditions they would be willing to accept your offer. In any case, you are taking the initiative. This way you prevent the other party from coming up with a concept that is not to your benefit.

It is even more important that you take the first initiative and make the first proposal when there are several parties included in the negotiation. During multilateral negotiations, there is always a proposal made by one of the parties that serves as the base. This proposal is usually the starting point for the rest of the negotiation. No matter what the final deal turns out to be, it usually resembles the initial agreement presented at the beginning.

Make allies

Many negotiators focus on the quantity and quality of their arguments, which requires a lot of preparation time. No matter how good your arguments are, there is no guarantee the negotiation will turn out in your favor. During negotiations, some people are just not convinced by arguments. They are more interested in views and opinions presented by specific individuals at the negotiation table. It is not necessarily *what* is said that counts. It's *who* says it.

During meetings with multiple parties, you're likely to have more impact when your viewpoint is supported by others, instead of laying more arguments on the table. Try to find possible allies prior to the meeting and explicitly ask them to support your arguments. In exchange, you can offer to support their viewpoints on other issues. By having an ally already from the beginning, you can tip the scales in your favor.

Find different negotiating parties

Your bargaining power immediately increases when you can negotiate with more than one party. If you wish to purchase a service and can choose from three suppliers, it's easier to reach an agreement with one supplier. You are no longer completely dependent on the one, and this immediately reduces their dominance on the other side of the negotiating table. No matter how good your relationship with your current negotiating partner is, it is wise to limit your dependence on them.

Come up with alternative proposals

Make sure that the outcome of a negotiation is not based on only one specific proposal. You'll strengthen your position when you can add several options. This way, you can influence the talks and stand a better chance of getting to a good outcome than less flexible negotiators who have can only propose one thing, or nothing. That puts the talks under pressure.

Start by having enough proxy

Too little or too much freedom can have a negative effect on your negotiating power. Not having enough proxy is limiting because you have too little authority to make concessions or explore new options. Moreover, you'll have to check with your backers continuously, and means that you will not be taken seriously by the other party.

On the other hand, having too much proxy can also be an disadvantage, because it can cause uncertainty with some negotiators, making them feel the responsibility lies entirely with them. They will constantly be wondering if the deal will be acceptable to their party.

Negotiations with an external party should start out with a thorough internal negotiation. Make sure you get a clearly defined mandate. Know your limitations, and know your options. Play down the high expectations the party you are representing might have and get them to think about possible alternatives. This prevents you from being sent to the negotiating table with only one proposal in your hand, and no alternatives.

Allow yourself enough time

For negotiating, do you have all the time in the world? Or are you under the gun? It makes a huge difference. Time is power. It can work in your favor, or it can work against you. Negotiators that are under pressure are usually more dissatisfied with the deal they negotiated than those who had more time. A negotiator under pressure has lower expectations of the end result, spends less time exploring options, and is more willing to make concessions, and go for a compromise.

Make sure time is not used against you. Do not negotiate when you're in a hurry or are discussing several items all at the same time. It directly weakens your position, and you'll come across uneasy and less composed. If the party you are representing have given you a deadline, assess whether making the deadline is more important than striking a good deal.

Expose them

There are negotiators that act dominant, or can be very intimidating. They come across as overly self-confident and seem sure of themselves when presenting their demands and arguments. They continuously interrupt you, talk loudly, and can even get personal.

And then there is the other type of negotiator, the one who

acts indifferent. He is the type that shows little or no interest in your arguments, is cordial, and seems completely unaffected, as if nothing matters to him. Both types aim to make you feel insecure, and set you off balance. For many, the natural response to this type of behavior is to ignore or imitate it. However, that won't work to your advantage. By acting like you are not effected by their behavior, you give them the upper hand. You might be thinking: "Apparently what I am doing does not work, so I will have to act tougher." Or, "I am unstoppable, let's see how far I can go with this." And if you're imitating the same dominant behavior, you run the risk of escalating the negotiation.

The most effective way to counteract a negotiator who is acting dominant is expose them: "Excuse me, but you're continuously interrupting me. I find that annoying." "Now I would like to finish my argument." Or, "You say you want to have a mutually beneficial outcome from these talks, but all of my demands have been disregarded. You can't have one without the other." Or, "You can continue to be very adamant in your demands, but if I did the same, we will never reach an agreement. Is that what you want?" By immediately calling out the other party for their dominant behavior, you let them know that you are on to their dirty trick.

Show them you're informed

Knowledge is power. People who seem to be an expert, get authority. People are more inclined to accept what an authority tells them than what a layman says. The less we know about a certain subject, the more we are likely to accept knowledge from an expert. Financial, legal, and technical experts are good at that. Experts in these fields give their customers advice with so much jargon that only few can really understand it. Opposing them is nearly impossible because we need all our wits to fully understand what is being said. This same principle also applies in negotiating. During the talks, the negotiator who is a specialist in a certain field that is being discussed will be taken seriously. And if there is no equivalent expert from the other party, any kind of opposing viewpoint is unlikely to be voiced.

Make sure you know your case extremely well. Don't let yourself be surprised with new facts and figures that you could have known beforehand. That way you let the other party know you are knowledgable. This will raise your status with the other party.

Show the other party from the start that you know what you are talking about. That way you present yourself as an expert, and that immediately adds to your stature at the bargaining table. However, don't overdo it. That usually evokes irritation, and puts the other party off. They are likely to think: "I can't follow him ... whatever."

In the case that you do not know enough to contribute to the discussion, you can always compensate your position by asking intelligent questions. Ask for facts, supporting arguments, and explanations. Don't be overwhelmed by an overkill of facts and figures. Don't let yourself feel insecure because you can't follow the enormous amount of information that is being presented. Let the other party know that you don't understand, or that you can't follow. "Do you think you can explain that again to me, this time by giving an example?" You can also opt to temporarily suspend the talks. That way you have time to study the information, and have it assessed by your own expert.

The carrot and the stick

Negotiations usually address certain legal, technical, social, organizational, and financial aspects. On an abstract level, you are also engaged in a personal power play. In this regard you have two power resources at your disposal: the carrot and the stick.

You use the carrot when you show the other party the benefits of your proposal: "With this campaign, you'll get the audience you want." Or, "By re-adjusting these regulations more people will qualify and your policy will be a bigger success." Or, "With this product, you can differentiate yourself from your competitors and increase sales by five percent."

Use the stick when you discuss the disadvantages of not accepting your offer. "You'll never make your target when you abandon the campaign." Or, "If you leave the legislation unchanged, then you'll hardly have any people qualify, and your policy will fail" or, "Without this product, you won't be able to distinguish yourself in the market and your sales will consequently decline."

By alternatively using the carrot and the stick during negotiations, you'll be able to see to which of the two the other party is sensitive. Is he enthusiastic about the advantages or uneasy about the disadvantages? After discovering this, you should adapt your argumentation and come up with substantiating evidence and alternative proposals.

As mentioned earlier, there should be a balance of power during a negotiation. When there is a substanticial difference, the stronger party will dominate the weaker one. For the time being it might seem to be beneficial to the stronger party, but on the long term it could have a negative impact. Take for example what banks and large financial institutions worldwide experienced in recent years. They thought they held all the cards when they negotiated with national governments, corporations, and the public.

The power of the banks was based on their enormous impact on the world economy. New York, London, Frankfurt, and Amsterdam sought favors from the banks because each city wanted to be the financial capital of the world, or at least to maintain their status. Each fought hard to make it easy for international banks and institutions to set up offices in their respective cities.

Besides that, corporations and companies had become accustomed to having a steady flow of credit from banks by issuing various financial products. These products were often so complicated that, with the exception of only a few financial experts, nobody really understood them. The steady line of credit gave banks and financial institutions a hold on corporations and companies. Not all banks knew how to cope with this newly claimed power. Bankers became hard negotiators, especially when they wanted to register in certain countries, which usually resulted in extremely beneficial conditions. Corporations and companies that had trouble meeting their interest payments were easily put under pressure. The enormous bonusses and salaries of bankers is a reflection of their dominance. When the financial crisis errupted, this was used against them. According to public opinion, the bankers had caused the financial crisis, and they deserved to be punished. Consequently, stricter regulation of the banking sector were passed that restricted banks and financial insitutions, and bankers were legally prosecuted. After years of arrogance, the banks had forfeited their crediability.

FIND OUT WHAT MAKES THE COUNTERPARTY TICK

Every negotiator has his or her own style. Each negotiator has specific traits and characteristics. Depending on the situation, most negotiators mix and match their negotiation skills and styles. No one ever applies the same approach in every situation. However, most negotiators have a preference for a certain approach. When a negotiation gets tense, a negotiator usually falls back on the approach he is the most comfortable with. When you recognize the different styles of negotiation, you'll be able to predict and influence their behavior. These are the most common styles of negotiation.

The dominant negotiator

The dominant negotiator acts alone and has no lack of self-confidence. He often takes charge of the talks, has excellent verbal skills when listing his demands and stating his arguments, and will not go out of the way for a confrontation. The dominant negotiator is assertive, and actively pushes for his desired outcome of the negotiation.

When you are dealing with a dominant negotiator, he usually acts like an alpha male and may even be aggressive. He dominates the conversation, threatens to terminate the relationship, and is very demanding.

Do's

The most effective way to deal with a dominant negotiator is to let him first state his arguments with plenty of time. Let him showboat his expertise, and when you do have criticism, direct it at his argument. Not at him personally.

When it's your turn to present your case, make sure you are confident and outline your arguments as professional as possible. Offer several proposals so that he has more than one to choose from. This way he still feels like he can influence the outcome.

Be positive when responding to specific aspects of his proposal or argumentation. Give him a feeling that he is gaining ground. That way you build up credit for later when concessions need to be made. Every now and then say "no". Just let him know that you don't agree with everything. That way he takes you seriously. Be strict when your boundaries have been passed.

"You say that you want to reach a beneficial outcome for both of us, but I don't see that happening during these talks ..."

"I would appreciate it if I would have the opportunity to explain my viewpoints ..."

"We've already made a concession, I haven't seen anything from your side yet ..."

Don'ts

There are also things you should never do when dealing with a dominant negotiator. Don't let yourself be constantly interrupted. Call him out when this happens: "Excuse me, I would appreciate it if you would let me first finish."

Never debate a dominant negotiator. He will want to prove he is right. Point out that where you both have differing viewpoints. By showing a slightest bit of submissiveness, you will automatically lose respect and run the risk that he will try to push his boundaries. Don't give him an inch of ground. And never be aggressive with him. It's a losing battle.

The rational negotiator

The rational negotiator has studied his case in-depth. He bases his decisions on facts, figures, and procedures. He is analytical and critical. He is objective and entertains alternatives. He thinks matters thoroughly through before making a decision. It is difficult to make an emotional connection with a rational negotiator because he keeps his distance. He guards his emotions.

Do's

The best way to negotiate with a rational negotiator is to be just as well-prepared. Communicate calmly and clearly and decide together with him which procedure you would like to follow.

Support your arguments with hard facts and figures. Be honest when presenting the pros and cons of each proposal. Let him know the information he will need to know before making a decision.

Allow him sufficient time to make a decision, and thoroughly discuss one or more alternatives with him. Negotiate content, not form.

Don'ts

Never put him under pressure. The rational negotiator needs time and information before making a decision. Never make emotional arguments, and don't try to act light-hearted. A composed, business-like approach is more congruent with his character. With the exception of showing your expertise and objective criteria, never try to dominate him. That will only irritate him. Resist the temptation to discuss a topic in great detail. That will only bog the negotiations down.

The hesitant negotiator

The hesitant negotiator comes across being neutral. It is hard to get a pulse on him. He doesn't say no, and he doesn't say yes. He's not a bad guy, but he's also not friendly. He constantly postpones making a decision, and is always asking for additional information. What does he really want?

One thing is for sure. The hesitant negotiator doesn't make decisions under pressure. He often says he needs to discuss it first with the people he is representing. He wants to hedge himself. It's difficult for him to take responsibility. He needs constant confirmation from his peers to take responsibility. During negotiations, the initiative will always be in your court, from the first meeting until the very end.

Do's

The most effective way to deal with a hesitant negotiator is talk calmly with them. Speak quietly, allow for silences, and regularly summarize the major points.

Ask lots of questions, specifically to find out what his doubts might be. With whom does he need to decide? Move back and forth between closed questions ("Do you need this statement deleted from the report?") and open questions ("What is your main objection to this proposal?"). Also vary between controled questions ("Do I understand correctly that price is especially important?") and solution-focused questions ("How much does extending the deadline meet your needs?").

Provide information that gives a sense of security. Give examples, with hard facts and figures.

Take regular breaks. Allow him time to reflect and to consult with others. Provide lots of information on paper so that they can re-read it later at their leisure. Put down intermediate points you've both agreed on in writing.

Don'ts

Don't set deadlines. The hesitant negotiator is likely to pull back.

Don't take his silence to mean consent. On the contary, it's a form of rejection. Don't try to dazzle him with a quick sales pitch. Then he'll back off immediately. Don't try to use your relationship with him as leverage. He won't find that appropriate in his way of making a decision.

The quiet negotiator

The quiet negotiator is the silent type. For him, words are golden. He speaks slow, and his sentences are curt. Each word is carefully weighed out. One-worded answers are not unusual, and words and sentences can be punctuated by long silences. The silent negotiator shows little or no emotion. And he certainly doesn't respond to your emotions.

Do's

The most effective way to deal with a quiet negotiator is to regularly include silences in your speech. Ask a lot of open questions and avoid those that can be answered with a simple "yes" or "no." After asking your question, patiently allow him to answer it. Have him elaborate on his answers. Ask for explanations or to give examples.

If his style of communiation makes the negotiation difficult, let him know. Ask him why there are so many silences and short answers to your questions. By letting him know that this form of negotiation makes it difficult to move forward, you can ask him what the cause might be. Take your time. Realize that every session with a quiet negotiator will be long, and there is likely to be many follow-up sessions. Indicate that you have plenty of time. Perhaps this will make him act faster.

Don'ts
Never start filling in his words during the silences. That makes it way too easy for the quiet negotiator. Don't reward his silence by making concessions.

Don't wait for the other person to talk. This will certainly not help both parties come to agreement.

The relational negotiator

The relational negotiator is friendly. He's open, approachable, and easy-going. He's interested in you and takes time for informal chit-chat. Sometimes it takes a while before getting down to business. He procrastinates on making tough decisions, and has difficulty when the other party is demanding. He can sometimes come across as being insecure. When you've won the trust of a relational negotiator, then he is loyal to the end of time.

Do's
Take time to make small talk with him. Be open and share per-

sonal matters with him. Talk about other things besides business. This reinforces the relationship and builds trust between the two of you.

Emphasize that you are both going to benefit from the negotiation. State regularly the importance of the relationship and envision how the future will be for both of you. Enquire now and then if his backers are going to support the proposal. Ask him how you can help him.

Don'ts

Don't jump the gun and get down to business right away. At the same time, don't get too caught up in too much idle banter. You're there to negotiate. Be careful not to make a concession too quickly because of the good relationship.

Don't act tough and business-like during the negotiations. Don't try to put him under pressure and don't make extreme demands. He'll see this as a sign that you don't think the relationship is important. Don't try to strip down his proposal. His backers will intervene and send another negotiator.

DIRTY TRICK
OUR STANDARD TERMS AND CONDITIONS

During the negotiations, the other party indicates that what you're asking goes against their company's terms and conditions. Therefore that issue is non-negotiable, and your objective is out of the question. You're likely to hear: "It's our company policy, and we can not deviate from company policy. You'll have to adapt your proposal to fit our standard terms and conditions."

The booking agent of a hotel is faced with a dilemma when he consults with a representative from a training company. The company wants to book two training rooms on different dates throughout the year. For the same dates, he wants to reserve rooms for twenty partiticipants who will be taking the training. The booking agent makes a good offer and says he is going to process the reservations. "The offer remains valid until a month before the actual training starts, then you'll have to let me know definitely," the booking agents says. Unfortunately, the representative from the training company can not agree with the booking agent: "According to our company's terms and conditions, we allow participants up to one week before the training date to cancel. We always ask our suppliers to comply with our conditions. I can't make any exceptions. Moreover, none of our suppliers has a problem with this." What should the booking agent do? It's a great booking but the hotel risks cancelations and not getting the training rooms and hotel rooms booked.

Just because something is standard for another party, doesn't mean that it's standard for you too. The term "standard conditions" is subjective.

Start by finding out if their conditions are really standard. Do they comply with their line of business, or are they only standard for that specific company? If the latter is the case, then carefully study the conditions and determine which ones are not beneficial to you. Take the time and do not make any hasty decisions. Have them studied by legal counsel.

Determine which clauses or conditions are or are not acceptable for you. Ask for compensation when you think your are being penalized by their standard company rules. Tell the other party that you also have "standard company conditions" that need to be considered (even if you haven't drafted them yet). Now you are procedurally equals again. Then ask them to meet you half way.

Keep in mind that this is a negotiation trick. If it is not in conflict with formal legislation or contradicts policy in your line of business, then standard conditions can also be applied to them.

DIRTY TRICK
MANIPULATING THE AGENDA

Manipulating the agenda can be done in various ways. For example, the negotiation can be bogged down from the start with an overloaded agenda. Or your important item has been planned till the very end. In both cases, the person who drafted the agenda knew that the longer the meeting takes, the less likely you'll be a tough negotiator at the end. By the end of the negotiation, you'll be tired and, for the sake of wanting to make headway, more likely to give in.

Another trick is picking an unfavorable timeslot to discuss your important item. That will usually be at the end of a long work week, before summer break or the end of the fiscal year, or perhaps just before an important deadline expires. The intention is to put you under pressure and cause stress. This works to their advantage.

A well-known example is the negotiations about the naming of the new car company that would result from the merger between Daimler-Benz and Chrysler. From the beginning of the negotiations, Jurgen Schrempf of Daimler Benz and Bob Eaton of Chrysler discussed the name of the new company. Schrempf wanted it to be called DaimlerChrysler and Eaton thought it should be called ChryslerDaimler. They were at a deadlock. Jurgen Schrempf suggested they discussed this matter later, and that other matters be discussed first such as equity ratios, management positions, and where the location of the new headquarters. After months of successful negotiations, these items were settled. The only pending matter was the name of the company. The talks resumed but immediately became deadlocked again. At that time, Jurgen Schremp threatened to call off the entire merger if the company would not be called DaimlerChrysler. Eaton had nothing to bargain with, and gave into Schrempf's demand.

If Schremper had tried that trick at the beginning of the negotiations, it would not have had any effect. But now the negotiations were in the final stages, there was too much at stake for Eaton not to give into Schremp's demand.

This type of manipulation can be avoided by setting the agenda yourself. If that is not possible, then ask for the agenda well in advance, and check the times, the number of subjects, and make sure to check when your items will be discussed. If you are given the agenda on the spot, take time to study it. Change the order of some items, and suggest removing those from the agenda that you think are unnecessary.

If you are getting tired during the talks, you can always request taking a break or postponing certain subjects to a later date.

DIRTY TRICK
THE DELAY TECHNIQUE

On a Tuesday morning a project manager discusses with a client the design requirements and the cost allocation of a test program. It concerns the implementation of an automation system. All is progressing well and it seems nothing stands in the way of the negotiations leading to a good deal. The project manager is encouraged by the progress of the negotiations and is starting to get high expectations. "I am extremely pleased with the way our meetings are going. If the talks go as smoothly and quickly about the distribution of costs as they did about design requirements, I'll have a day off tomorrow, and I can do some sight-seeing. I'll only need Friday to touch base with the board."

To his surprise the mood at the talks goes sour after a while. All of a sudden, every detail needed to be discussed at great length and in great detail, while at the beginning of the negotiation those details were taken for granted. Also his client is frequently interrupted by his telephone during the talks. This takes a lot of time. To the manager's dismay, the client is unable to make any agreement by Tuesday, and Wednesday does not look promising either.

By Thursday afternoon, the project manager is getting restless. After almost a week of negotiations, he is going to have to report back to the board with nothing. Most likely now, he will have to offer more concessions if he is going to have any results by the end of the week.

By revealing his planning to the other party, the project manager got himself in a bind. Friday was his deadline to present his deal to the board of directors. While initially time played no role in the negotiations, suddenly there was a deadline. This proved to be a powerful leverage for the other party.

A deadline limits the time negotiators have to talk, and makes time a factor. Never let the other party know that you have a time limit. Suddenly the other party will take all the time it needs and delay the talks. When there is little time left, you'll be obliged to make concessions because you need to see some results.

If the other party knows you have a deadline, then act as if it is not that important. "I would prefer to have this finalized before October, I am more interested in having it done well than having it done by a certain deadline." Or, "I see that we are not going to finish before Friday. Therefore, I will cancel my flight and book a room for the weekend. Can I suggest we resume our talks on Saturday?" As soon as they notice that the deadline is flexible, and you are willing to negotiate longer, the other party will suddenly become more receptive.

Are you aware of the time of day when you are most alert and fit? Will the meeting be on Friday afternoon 3pm, which will be your fourth meeting of the day? Are you negotiating at the end of a fiscal quarter, or just before the holiday season, or at the end of the calendar year? Do you know if the other party has already met its target or can use the additional revenue?

DIRTY TRICK
THE TRAP

A negotiator who has invested a lot of time into a negotiation is more likely to make a concession than someone with whom you just started negotiating.

A management consultant sits at the negotiation table with a potential client for the sixth time. From the five consultancy agents that were asked to submit a proposal, her agency was selected after two rounds. After five previous meetings with the potential client, her initial enthusiasm has ebbed away because no agreement has been finalized yet. Everytime they are close, the client requests further clarification, or additional amendments to be added or excluded. In the meantime, four months have passed since the first tender was submitted.

Again and again the project manager from the management consultant says: "we're almost there." And then adds: "It's only that we think that the hourly rate and the headcount of consultants is too much. That exceeds our budget, and in times like these, it sends the wrong message to the rest of the company. We kindly request that you make these adjustments according to our wishes, and give us

*a new quote. There is nothing standing in the way of coming to an
agreement."*

*What do you do now? Giving into their demands might easily
mean that you don't get anything out of the deal. If you had known
these demands from the beginning, you probably would have never
submitted a tender. But as this stage, calling off the negotiations
doesn't seem like a good option.*

Negotiators want to cut their losses. They are more likely
to walk away from a negotiation at the beginning than at the
end. A lot of valuable time and effort have already been invested in the talks. They need to be reimbursed. As long as a party
has suffered from a commerical loss, the negotiator prefers to
make the most out of a negotiation. Something is better than
nothing. Some negotiators use this to their advantage. They
know already in advance that some of their demands will be
objected to, and that if they introduce these at the beginning of
the talks, the other party is likely to walk away. By prolonging
the negotiations and presenting the difficult demands towards
the end of the negotiation, the sly negotiator knows that the
other party is not likely to walk away from the negotiation table
with nothing. After all, the other party has invested a lot of
time and effort into the talks.

In this situation, you can defend yourself by sticking to your
guns. Afterall, the other party has also a vested interest in the
negotiations, and doesn't want to leave empty handed either.
You can also request additional conditions to the agreement.
In the above example, the management consultant can also

demand that the minutes for the various negotiation rounds be documented because they are not included in the numerous hours of negotiating. By introducing your own last-minute demands, you bring back the balance in the negotiation. "If you want us to pay a penalty if we don't meet the deadline, then we demand reward when we deliver on time. That is reasonable. We can also decide to drop both requirements. What would you like?"

DIRTY TRICK
THE REPLACEMENT

Replacing negotiators is a known trick to offset the other party. Unexpectedly, a negotiator has a new person sitting in front of him who he does not know. That often changes the scope of negotiation. Instead of addressing the planned issues, all of a sudden the focus has changed towards the relationship. The purpose of switching negotiators is to force the other party to be more receptive because if he does not, he threatens the good relationship and negotiations.

For many years, you have had a good rapport negotiating with the same agent. Now you plan on meeting him at an annual convention. You are going to discuss the annual price increases and change in volume. You arrive at the convention and to your surprise and disappointment, you find out that he is not there, and that you have to talk with his supervisor and a representative from procurement. Suddenly, they want to study the agreement carefully because they have received other offers. If you still want to close a deal for this year, most likely you'll not be able to propose an annual price increase. In fact, you might even have to lower your price. Instead of what you thought would be a friendly chat has turned into a serious negotiation with two high-powered negotiators who are questioning the relationship.

How do you deal with this? To start, avoid making quick concessions. That's what they expect you to do. For one, let them know that you expected to meet with someone else and that you have not prepared for the last minute changes in the meeting. This gives you time to readjust your approach and position in the meeting. Ask the new negotiators what their needs and priorities are. If one of them asks to elaborate on the substance of your proposal, let them know that you think the relationship and content of the agreement are important and need more time to draft an appropriate offer.

4

THE EXPLORATION PHASE

The discussion phase will hopefully have made clear where your priorities lie and where concessions need to be made. Now it's time for a new phase. No matter how far you have already gone, avoid the urge to close the deal. Take up a new position and see what more is possible. This is called the exploration phase. This phase allows you to explore new possibilities, entertain new options and alternatives, and come up with compromises.

REACHING AGREEMENT

The following tactics will help you get closer to your desired outcome.

Start the negotiation with the small stuff

First talk about the items that you most likely will agree on. Start with the items you are least interested in, and are not very important to you. By easily getting to a consensus on these matters, you build trust and establish a good basis for constructive negotiation.

Bench conflicting viewpoints

Don't let a conflicting interest stall the progress of the negotiations. Put the matter temporarily aside and continue pursueing reconciling interests.

When you feel a specific issue is sensitive and emotions are getting heated, change the talks to another matter and discuss it at a later time when emotions have cooled down.

Use a basic proposal

What do you agree to? Establish shared interests and find common ground. From here, you can reach a broad-scoped proposal, based on what everyone agrees to. Subsequently, each party can add their own needs and requirements to the proposal.

The exploration phase is the most effective when each party acknowledges the additions and special requirements of the other side, instead of criticizing them. This way both are working on a mutual proposal and emphasize what they agree upon. This brings both parties closer together and the differences become increaslingly smaller.

Stick to shared principles or criteria

Negotiators can also determine the outcome, based on criteria that both agree upon. Instead of trying to convince each other with arguments, that might be subjective or objective, they can also base the outcome on shared criteria, or principles, as a standard. Here are are a few examples:

- legislation (abiding to what the law stipulates);
- financial ratios (the price may not exceed ten per cent);
- price indicators (the price must be equal to the average market growth);

- principles, norms and values (no one should lose out).

This way negotations will be more rational and objective. Note, there is a chance that a lot of time will be spent determing the criteria. The legitimacy and choice of the criteria are an important part of the negotiation. A negotiator must realize that in this stage of negotiations the outcome might be determined by the norm.

Negotiate horizontally instead of vertically

If you can, negotiate multiple topics at the same time. Do not discuss each interest separately, but deal them all together. As a package, you can ask your partner which part gets priority.

For example, two parties are negotiating the development of a sustainable treatment plant. They need to negotiate three major components: the price, the terms of delivery, and warranty.

If they would negotiate vertically, they would first start with the price, then the terms of delivery, and finally end with the warranty. It is very likely that they will meet "in the middle" for each item. Both sides will make concessions and will only lead to across the board compromises. Each side will have made compromises on all three components and neither would have gotten what they came for. Both sides would lose out.

Now, if both parties would negotiate horizontaly, then they could establish which items would be the most important for either of them. This way, each side is more likely to come to agreement with optimal results for their important interests, and compromises on the lesser ones.

The negotiating environment

The inexperienced negotiator will sometimes approach negotiations like going into battle, and think it is a matter of "winning or losing." Parties will act arrogant, will make hard demands, and show little interest in the views and interests of the other. When the other side is not acknowledged, the talks become riddled with distrust and irritation. The atmosphere is ruined when both parties don't want the other party to gain anything. That is why it is important to keep the relationship constructive. Successful negotiations are usually the ones where both sides don't want the other one to lose out on anything.

Improve the talks by showing interest in the other party and acknowledging their motives and interests.

Acknowledge the interests of the other side

Instead of opposing each other, start the negotations by expressing interest in the needs of the negotiating partner. This shows that you want the negotiations to succeed, for them and for you.

For example, show the importance of flexibility:

"I understand that you want to have flexibility in the trainings included in our agreement. I also think that we need to ensure this as much as possible."

But you need to restrict how much the other party's demands can be implemented, and negotiate it like this:

"And that is why you want to have a cancellation period of two weeks, but I think that's asking too much. I suggest a period of one month."

This approach has a positive impact at the negotiation table. You create a sincere feeling of wanting to cooperate. You show that you are willing to cooperate and that you want to see everyone's interests met. This does not mean that you are a weaker negotiator that easily caves in. On the contrary, for implementing the issues you will obviously, still need to do some hard bargaining.

Ask more questions

By asking questions you will show that you are interesed in the other party. Also, you won't be taken by surprise later, during the discussions by other interests that need to be considered. By asking questions, the other side secs that you are taking them seriously. In addition, asking questions gives them the opportunity to explain their views. This makes them feel they have been understood, and then they are more open to listening to your story.

Asking many questions has an additional advantage. It shows that you are genuinely interested. Job applicants who ask many questions during a job interview come across as stronger candidates than those who just talk about themselves and tell about what they have done. Inquisitive candidates seem smarter and are generally perceived to be more sympathetic.

Loosen up

You're negotiating, not playing poker. The time when a negotiator was absolutely not allowed to show any emotions is long gone. A party that doesn't show any emotions, makes it very uncomfortable for the other one.

Someone that doesn't show any emotions, makes it extremely uncomfortable for the others. The other side is probably thinking "what does he think about what I am offering?" Or, "I don't get him." These thoughts don't contribute to an open dialogue. Show your emotions in small doses, and your thougths and ideas strengthen your contact with the other. Giving and receiving feedback is useful to both parties. That way, everybody knows what the other likes. Approaching it from that angle, the negotiation will work to everyone's advantage. Being flexible during the negotiations contributes to a more open atmosphere.

Focus on common ground

You increase your chances of getting a positive outcome when you focus on similarities instead of concentrating on the differences. By regularly acknowledging the things and interests you both agree on, you strengthen the mutual ground and sense of interdependence. This will result in a feeling of working "shoulder to shoulder" at reaching a mutual goal. This approach is very different to hammering away on conflicting viewpoints. Then the gap between the two only widens.

In international diplomacy, when both parties are at complete opposites of the spectrum, talks need to start at the very ground level and in good setting. For example, the relations between North Korea and the U.S. are anything except warm. It would seem that any kind of negotiation between both parties is bound to fail. In recent years, official negotiations between the two Koreas, the U.S., China, Japan, and Russia on dismantling North Korea's nuclear program have been in an impasse. In November 2013, representatives from all sides have entered into a new series of informal talks to resolve the nuclear standoff. If formal talks were held, both parties would be put under the pressure of international media coverage. In the social context of informal talks at undisclosed locations, the parties can then easily enter into dialogue and voice their options and needs without any external influences. So far all the parties involved have warmed up and have touched on issues pertaining to bilateral relations.

Most of the time people don't pay much attention to the atmostphere during negotiations. During negotiation talks, the atmosphere is often strained by:

- Criticizing the other's arguments and consequently causing more irritation.
- 'I understand your standpoint, but ...': Everything that has been said before "but" has been deleted from the discussion.

- Constantly interrupting each other and thinking that you know what the other party means before they have fully explained themselves. In doing so, you give the other party the impression that you don't take them seriously.
- Asking suggestive questions: 'Don't you think your demands are unreasonable?'
- Talking most of the time: nothing is more tiresome than listening to someone who dominates the conversation. The counterparty will get bored. It's not all about you, the other party is just as important.
- Getting personal. Don't get negative and put down the other side, however tempting it might be. Discuss what the other party brings up and leave personalities out of it. A remark like "You probably don't have much experience in this area" will not create a good relationship. Try to communicate with the other person in a positive way. For example: "I get the impression that I am not clear, is that right?" Or, "from your remark, I get the feeling that you don't see that happening, is that correct?"

DIRTY TRICK
THE BOGEYMAN

The other side lets you know that your proposal is attractive and reasonable. "But unfortunately, I don't have the resources to take you up on it. I would like to, but I just can't." By showing appreciation for your product, service or proposal, they communicate to you that it is outside of their influence to take you up. Rationally, they agree with your proposal and would actually love to take the deal offered to them. But they can't due to outside circumstances.

The term "bogey" is used in the game of golf, and in the military. In the context of negotiating this term refers to a target, a false target, or a decoy.

What should you do? Initially, you're probably flattered by the compliment about your product, service or proposal. Flattery weakens everybody at the knees. Now take caution and don't give in right away. Let the other party know you sympathize with them and give them time to come up with other solutions. Then, suspend the negotiations.

If they don't get back to you, even after suspending your talks, you might consider making some concessions, granted they make a few as well. If they can't meet you, then you can adapt your offer to what the other side has to offer.

DIRTY TRICK
THE BETTER OFFER

Your proposal is dismissed with a casual "I have a better deal than what you are offering me." Their intention is clear: you better come up with something better than that. You've been put under pressure to accomodate to the other side. This kind of "pressuring" is commonly used to banks when small businesses request a loan.

"Your competitor is giving me a better deal, while you are my

preferred banker! He's offering both a better commission and interest rates. You turned out to be a disappointment. Is that how you treat all your customers?"

"You've put me in a difficult position. Because we've known each other already so long, I would prefer to do business with you, but your quote doesn't compare with the one that I got from another bank. I wouldn't be a good business man if I didn't take their offer. I'll give you one more chance to come up with a better deal."

And there you are, the poor account manager, who doesn't want to jeopardize the relationship and risk losing a customer. How do you solve this problem?

Well, if the customer has a better deal, why is he telling you about it? Chances are he is bluffing, and just wants to put you under the gun. Probably there are others quotes but they are not much better than what the other side is making them out to be.

Ask to see the other proposals so you can come up with something better. If the other party is bluffing, they will expose themselves. But if the other side really has a better offer, you can consider making a few concessions and determing your bottom price. If the other party offers a much better deal, he should by all means take it. But always determine your bottom price. If you have reached that already, it's time to stop.

DIRTY TRICK

THE GOOD AND BAD NEGOTIATOR

This is the "good cop and bad cop" version of negotiating. You got the gist of it already. You are dealing with a party that sends two representatives: the blunt or tough guy, and the friendly, reasonable one. Many *think* they can see through this trick, but are usually *had* at the end.

They usually act confident to the "bad guy negotiator" but allow themselves to be sucked in by the good guy and respond by being mild because, *after all*, he seems to be reasonable. That makes the "good negotiator" actually the more dangerous of the two. Would you really have liked the bid from the good negotiator if the bad guy hadn't been there? Don't let yourself be conned:

1. Act indifferent to both the bad guy and good guy negotiator.
2. Let them know that you don't like the way everyhing has gone. This shows your insight in how things are developing and that you are confident.
3. Determine the offer from the good guy separately from the one offered from the bad guy. That way you can figure out if the offer is acceptable.

The principle of the good and the bad negotiator works because it creates a contrast. By first hearing an unattractive proposal, the following seems a lot better. Then you're hooked.

Recruitment agencies often work with this concept. Clients receive a selection of three candidates. One of the three does not fit the job description at all, but is still included. The reason for this is that the other two candidates, who might not entirely meet all the criteria, seem a lot better than the "least likely" candidate. Without the contrast, the other two would probably be disappointing.

5

BARGAINING

Concessions are part of the game. Differences will always remain despite exploring other possibilities and proposals. However, be cautious when making concessions.

The negotiations about a merger between two companies have entered into a crucial phase. It must be determined at this stage which departments of each company are redundant so that unnecessary costs can be reduced. In several aspects departments overlap too much, which increases the costs. The talks start getting tougher. The negotiator from company A wants to show goodwill and makes a concession. "We are ready to close our distribution department, but I would appreciate it if we could keep our administation department. The negotiator from company B expresses little or no emotion. "Your distribution department was redundant anyway. You would have had to close it down anyway and farm it out. Our admin is perfect and we are not at all interested in yours." This is not what the negotiator from company A had anticipated. Instead of getting some kind of credit by taking the first step and making the first sacrifice, the other party carelessly walks all over him and his offer. Moreover, he is left holding the short end of the stick.

The content of the concession is usually not important. It's *when* the concession is made. Timing is everything. Hold off before making a concession until the other party asks for one. It's a common *faux pas* of unexperienced negotiators to give away concessions before they were ever asked.

THE CONCESSION GAME

The following rules of thumb will increase your effectiveness when making concessions.

Wait as long as possible with a concession

Don't be too quick to make a concession. The other party will start to expect that they can get more out of you. They might think you have raised your stakes too high, and will quickly adjust your requirements. Moreover, they will get the idea that you can't handle pressure and can't hold out long. Therefore, they will also think that you are prepared to make many more concessions. Hold off on making concessions until the end when the negotiations might be getting tough and when a concession has the greatest impact.

Making a concession while going through a hard negotiation or almost at a deadlock is valuable. It puts the negotiation back on track and sends out a good vibe. Besides that, as a negotiator it makes you feel good too. After all, you've accomplished something. The other party fought hard for the concession, and feels he had to go to great extremes. Neither of you would have any of these emotions if a concession had been thrown in from the start.

Limit the number of concessions

However tempting it might be to offer many small bite-sized

concessions, this strategy is not recommended. If you're dealing with a negotiator who is out to get all he can, then this strategy will cost you dearly. He will only ask you to make more. Everytime you reward him with a concession, he will only want more. By being frugal and only making significant concessions, you'll stop the momentum from the other negotiator who constantly demands more concessions. By limiting your concessions, you strengthen your bargaining position and come across as more credible.

Exaggerate your concessions

When you make a concession, make it extremely clear to the other party that you've made a huge gesture on your part. The other party might not perceive it that way, but you can always exaggerate just to give them the idea. When bargaining, remember that it is not only the content of your concession that really matters. It's the fact that you are making a concession. Everything is marketing, and that also applies to bargaining. Give them your Oscar-winning performance when you make a concession. For example, don't say, "we've agreed to extend the payment period from 30 to 60 days." But rather, "In a long, heated meeting with management, I fought tooth and nail to get your payment extended an additional 30 days." Take some liberties: better to overdo it, than to play it down. Save modesty for another occasion. Give the other party the impression that it is costing you a rib, otherwise they are not likely to acknowledge that you are really making a significant concession.

Tit for tat

Before making a concession, always ask for something in return. Or better yet, request something specific from their side. In essence, negotiation is only exchanging priorities with each other. If the other party really wants you give up something, then what is he willing to trade for it? Mutual exchange applies here: "I might be willing to give up this if you ..."

In exchange for a concession, you can also ask the other party to accept the deal at the same time. Then you're done negotiating.

Make a conditional concession

It is advisable to make a concession under condition. This can be in a variety of ways. For one, you can indicate that you are willing to accept their demands, provided you'll be compensated while the next items in the negotiation is being discussed. Or you offer concessions under condition that the entire package is acceptable.

Another variation includes taking the other party's request under condition: "I'll consider your proposal if it is feasible." Or, "I'll discuss your offer internally and see if I can get it accepted." These statements don't commit you to anything, but they are a token of goodwill.

Ask them for a concession

Of course, you can also request them to make a concession. It might seem obvious but a lot of times negotiators forget that they can also make requests from the other party. This is especially the case when the other party is fighting hard for significant demands. Now is the best time to ask what you want. But ask for more than what you really want. Put your request out there and see if they become silent. Sometimes this silence creates the right moment to get a concession from the other party.

Even though you might not even be out for a concession, ask for one anyway. This creates the right mood for offering concessions. You can also mention a previous request that had not been honored. This will also be seen on your part as a concession.

Saying "no" occasionally

Give and take is part of the game. But that doesn't necessarily mean that everytime they ask, you give. Say "no" once in a while to their requests. Or demand something in return. Especially on issues that are important to you, it is essential that you clearly show your boundaries, and what you are willing and unwilling to accept. Occasionally saying no gives the other party clarity and strengthens your credibility. It helps the other party find out where you stand.

Keep a concession in your back pocket

Have at least one spare concession incase the negotiation runs aground. Offering this concession will have a big impact and get the negotiations back on track. Be careful not to say, "this is my last concession." Or, "this is my final offer." When you do, you don't have anymore bargaining chips and have lost control over the negotiations. You hand over control of the meetings to the other party. If they don't take you up on your concession, they will never believe you again when you try to make another concession.

DIRTY TRICK
SALAMI TACTICS

This dirty trick refers to a salami sausage sliced into thin pieces. Cut off a thin slice of sausage and there is almost an entire salami still left. You might think, "There's nothing to worry about." During negotiations, the other party will ask you to make numerous small concessions. Considering you still got a way to go, it won't seem like that much of a concession to make. However, it never is just one small concession. This tactic is also known as the "piecemeal strategy." During the course of negotiations, the other party will continuously ask little by little for more and more. Each concession doesn't seem like much, but together they slowly add up, and pretty soon your whole salami is gone.

An account manager of a bank negotiates with a CFO of a timber mill about a line of credit. In addition to negotiating the interest rate, they also need to discuss brokerage fees, installment payments, collateral, and insurance.

Considering the stiff competition, the bank has given the timber mill a competitive quote. The CFO goes through the terms of the agreement thoroughly with the account manager from the bank. When they get to the interest rate, the CFO says he thinks its on the high side. "This should be lower, not much, but the rate is actually lower. I agree to the credit spread of 60 points instead of 80." After presenting arguments back and forth, the account manager suggests a spread of 70 points. Considering the entire deal, he could justify making a concession. But the meeting isn't over yet. When they get to the commission, the account manager is asked to show a little goodwill. " You can surely shave off the commission fee a little bit?" Again, the account manager gives in and reduces the commission fee because he could drop it a little more. But the two are far from finished. The CFO continues, "before I agree, I would like the premium on treasury products slightly reduced. If you lower the premium by a few points, we have a deal." Hesitantly, the account manager agrees because he doesn't want the negotiation to fail due to a few minor points.

However, when the deal needs to be approved by the bank's credit committee, they are not satisfied. For the bank, the security offered and the performance of the credit are too great a risk, and the deal is turned down.

Never negotiate components of a deal one by one. Discuss

the issues in their entirety. That way it is easier to "swap" concessions back and forth, and prevents you from piecemealing each item individually.

Emphasize to the other party that they are asking you to make a major concession. If you easily accommodate their request, you ruin your own bargaining power. In other words, they are not asking for a small token, they want a significant one.

When they start asking again for a minor concession, let them know that you see a pattern, and it's not what you want. This lets them know you are on to them.

Always ask something in return for a concession. No matter how small, make sure you get something back. It can be a concession from the other party, but it might just be the last thing needed to close the deal.

DIRTY TRICK

ESCALATING DEMANDS

There are several variations to the dirty trick of escalating demands. The most common is when the other party creates a dilemma for you. You ask the other party to make a concession, and they respond by making the conditions or requirements of another component of the negotiation tougher. An improvement to one part of the deal means you lose out on another part of it.

The next one is more aggressive. The other party makes an offer. If you do not immediately agree, they step up the conditions. On top of that, they tell you that the offer is only good for a limited time. Logically, the best thing to do is accept the offer. The purpose of escalating is to put you under pressure. The other party wants you to lower your expectations, and quickly accept the deal they just offered you.

What do you do? Don't be impulsive. Take time to think about the unexpected factors that have come up. If you respond too quickly, chances are you will lose out.

Say for example, that this is not the way you want to do business. Just let the talks slide into deadlock. That way, you let the other party know you won't be pressured. If there is a meeting room nearby, allow the other party to discuss among themselves where they can come up with another offer that is more appealing to you.

6

DEADLOCK AND FINALIZING THE DEAL

I've said it before and I'll say it again. We believe that ..."
Or, "I don't see us getting any closer to an agreement. I'll make one more concession because we're not getting anywhere like this."

These are two common responses when a negotiation is not making any headway. Despite proposals and concessions there is often a moment when parties are not moving towards a deal. What do you do next?

Inexperienced negotiators are often frightened of deadlock and will avoid it at all costs. Veteran negotiators on the contrary make effective use of deadlocks. They consider it a tool for getting closer to closing a deal.

THE PURPOSE OF DEADLOCK

There are two ways most negotiators head off a deadlock: by endlessly repeating their arguments, or by handing over a concession. In both cases, the negotiator considers the deadlock as something to avoid because it leads to confrontation and causes tension between the two parties. However, deadlocks can have several positive effects on negotiations.

Deadlock is a sign of communication

Instead of giving a concession you can let the talks run into a deadlock. That way you communicate to the other party where your boundaries are, and that they should not expect anything more from you.

Test the other party's backbone

Negotiators often wonder if they have struck a good deal and negotiated enough. Could they have gotten more? If a negotiator never let the talks go into deadlock, most likely they have never tested their own negotiation skills to the fullest. They consider deadlock to be a sign of failure. On the contrary, it's a tactical way to test the perservence of the other party. How much will he hold his ground during deadlock? Does he buckle, or does he stick to his guns? During deadlock, let the initiative come from the other party. Wait for their response. This is a good indication of the situation.

Deadlock forces creativity

If negotiators are stubborn but still need each other, then they look for alternatives. They have to entertain new solutions and perspectives, and come up with new ideals if they want to make an agreement.

DEADLOCKS MAKE THE FINAL DEAL SWEET

To be satisfied with the final deal, the negotiator has to believe that he had gone out on a limb to make the deal happen. By giving the other party a run for its money, the negotiator will appreciate the deal he negotiated much better than if the other party agreed to everything without a fight.

A couple walks into the showroom of a car dealership. They want to buy a new car and wonder how much they can get for their old one. The car salesman asks, "What did you have in mind?" The woman replies, "Ten thousand dollars." The salesman who believes that the car is worth more yells out, "Deal." The woman thinks silently to herself "That was too easy, I can get more for my car." She says, "Let me sleep on it."

If the salesman had waited a little bit longer and made a lower counteroffer, the couple would have felt much better with their offer and wouldn't have withdrawn it.

It's not only the result of the deal that matters, it's also the perception of how the results were achieved that are important. The other party has to feel like they got the most out of the deal, otherwise they will be left with a lingering dissatifaction.

Deadlock helps "sell" the deal to your backers

Deadlock is an important instrument in selling the agreement to the party the negotiator represents. The headquarters should also feel satisified with the deal that has been negotiated for them. Again, it's not only the content of the deal that matters. It's also the way the deal was hammered out. A deal that was quickly sealed will often raise many questions by your backers. They will think that the negotiator did not make a strong enough case when representing their interests.

If you are the negotiator for your party, chances are you'll be sent back to re-negotiate a deal if you first come home with a quick one. Then you are likely to have a counterparty that is armored to the teeth. A deadlock could have easily prevented this from happening.

PITFALLS DURING DEADLOCK

During negotiation deadlock has a clear purpose. However, when the deadlock is not used correctly you run the risk that talks will ultimately fail. To avoid that from happening, the following steps should be observed.

Repeating arguments

Avoid statements such as: "I would again like to emphasize that ..." Or, "I would like to say again ..." Repeating arguments made earlier does not move the negotiation forward and is more likely to cause irritation. Most likely the other party won't listen and they will become indifferent.

Giving in too soon

Many negotiators feel uneasy about a deadlock. The tension rises and the outcome becomes uncertain. They think, "Don't let the negotiations fail." Many times negotiators think the only way to prevent deadlock is by accomodating the other party with a quick concession. A concession from your side is one of the possibilities to smooth things over and get talks back on track. And there is nothing wrong with that. But if it becomes a pattern in which you are continually the one making concessions, you should start to ask yourself if you are too complaisant, and wonder if the other party is taking advantage of it.

A good alternative is to test the other party and let them come up with a concession or new solution. Maybe they will make a concession and an offer. If not, as a last resort you can always make a concession. The impact will be greater if you hold out with the concession, than if you give it up in an early stage.

Threatening

Of course, you can point out to the other party what the negative consequences will be if no agreement is made. However, when these tactics start to resemble blackmail, you're entering the realm of improper negotiation techniques and treading on unsavory ground.

But even if the tricks are not illegal, it's better to walk away from negotiations with a clear conscious, and not resort to such practices. When you do that, it limits the other party as well as yourself. If your threats backfire, you lose face, and most importantly your credibility. If the other party takes your threat seriously and acts upon it, most likely he will pull back later.

Being independent

Putting on a poker face. Giving the others the impression that you don't care whether or not the negotiation comes to an agreement. This trick also applies when you want the other party to make a move and break the stalemate. This tactic is effective in bridging gaps between two parties. This will come in handy later, especially when you're dealing with a tough negotiator.

Blame the other guy

"What you are proposing is unreasonable." Or, "Can you be more constructive?" By using these statements, you put the blame on the other party and demand a solution from them. This way you disqualify the other negotiating partner and instill the idea that they are the only ones who can end the deadlock. Avoid getting personal and making accusations. This will only lead to irritation and won't help reach an agreement. Instead of making general accusations and using words like "unreasonable" and "non-constructive", it's better to give concrete examples and expectations. "Your demand to tighten the margin of error to half a percent of the technical limits, that's asking too much ". Another example is, "I don't recognize any of our interests and objectives in your arguments." Or, "can you come up with an alternative proposal that clearly includes our viewpoints?"

BREAKING DEADLOCK

There are tricks to effectively maintain a deadlock. It's important to realize that a deadlock is not a situation that should be shunned. On the contrary, a deadlock can be a productive phase when negotiations continue. If done correctly, it can influence the final outcome in a positive way.

State the status quo and suspend the negotiations

If you have the idea that both parties are not getting any closer to reaching an agreement, and no new information is presented, it's time to summarize the status quo, and suspend the proceedings. Decide when you want to meet again. Ask each other to consider new alternatives and concessions they would be willing to make. Contact each other in the period before the next meeting and discuss which steps need to be made before getting to an agreeement. Communicate this information with your team so they can consider it as well. The other negotiator is likely to do the same with his backers in which they can also come up with new solutions and alternatives. The next time you meet each other at the negotiation table, you both can exchange your new ideas.

Suspending the talks allows you and the other party time to reconsider and come up with new solutions. Especially when negotiations become heated and emotional, it allows time for both parties to reflect. The suspension allows you time to discuss with your headquarters and consider questions such as "do we want to have deal as it stands now? Or do we prefer to have no deal?" Or, "are there other possibilities that have been overlooked? What kind of concession do we want to see in return?" The answers to these questions will break the deadlock. If they don't, then at least you know where you stand. It is up to you (or your headquarters) to decide. Postpone further talks, accept the last offer or let the negotiation take its own course.

Point out alternatives

What is the alternative if no deal is made? Should you compromise? Or explore the consequences if the standoff continues. To what extent is this preferable to a concession from both sides, or coming up with an alternative?

Obviously, its best to do this before you even start talks. If this proves beneficial to you, go for it. If the other party has one or more alternatives, it doesn't mean you have to take them up on it.

Replace negotiators

Sometimes it's the personalities of the negotiators that get in the way. Both sides cause mutual irritation, afraid of losing face. Or it's just plain bad or limited negotiating skills. All these factors can cause a negotiation to slide into deadlock. When negotiators and members of a negotiation team are replaced, this changes the chemistry of the talks. It's a good way to get discussions going again. New negotiators usually want to prove themselves and will do the utmost within their mandate to make sure the negotiations succeed. Because of their willingness to get the talks headed in the right direction, new faces at the negotiation table bring fresh ideas and new perspectives. Perhaps they'll come up with an original or modified proposal which the previous negotiation team had not thought of.

Sometimes changing the location of the talks helps get negotiations out of a rut. For a change, instead of meeting at your office, meet at a neutral location, or even at the office of the other party. By changing the location, you show the other party that you are still committed to getting past the deadlock. Here too applies the principle of mutuality. Now, it's their turn to do something to break the deadlock.

Only let the leaders lead

When negotiation teams run into deadlock, it is best to let the leaders of the team to negotiate further. Too many people at the table complicates everything. Less people involved, means fewer differing opinions and standpoints to be ironed out.

One on one negotiation simplifies the talks, but means more responsibilty for the negotiaton leaders. However, that's not necessarily a bad thing. Negotiators want to show they are leaders, capable of successfully closing a deal. Sometimes the pressure finalizing a deal is so great that formal meetings don't help. Informal meetings offer an ideal opportunity to discuss alternatives without the tension and expectations of formal discussions. Negotiators can get anchored to the official meeting rooms and feel too much pressure. A solution is to change the setting and meet in an informal surrounding. This shows your intention of wanting the negotiations to succeed.

Elaborate on the points that you agree

Negotiation is easier when you focus on your mutual goals. Instead of emphasizing contentious issues, highlight the areas you agree on. By shifting the discussion to the topics you agree, the negotiations will be more constructive. Moreover, the part that you mutually agree upon becomes more significant for the negotiations. Consequently, it becomes more difficult for confliciting positions to sabotage the negotiations.

By temporarily putting the conflicting issues on hold and addressing the ones that both parties stand to benefit from, a mutual package is created. In the scheme of the negotiation, an issue that once caused so much conflict starts to pale in light of the greater benefit of the entire deal.

Developing alternative proposals is another version. Instead of creating a deal based on everyone's initial viewpoint, you can develop a new proposal together. This can be a completely new proposal, or you can start with a basic concept and elaborate together while adding new ideas. The advantage is that you both feel like you "own" the mutual proposal. Both parties are no longer sitting at opposite ends of the negotiation table. On the contrary, they stand shoulder to shoulder.

Let time do its work

Negotiations take time. Ideas and proposals have to mature in the minds of negotiators. People have to get used to the idea that they will leave with less than what they had anticipated.

Make a concession

The easiest way to break a deadlock is to make a concession. You've made an offer, now it's the other party's turn. Of course, you can only make a concession if you have room to bargain, that's why it's important to have some cards up your sleeve.

Time for a compromise

When deadlock is broken, parties are often ready to make a compromise. Usually this consists of a package of specific points that both parties have already agreed on. The compromise is based on various previous phases of the negotiation that the parties have gone through. Quite often after a first round of opening moves, discussions, exploration, negotiation, concessions and deadlocks follows a new round of the same.

It's good to know when you have gotten the most out of negotiations. If you think that the proposal on the table is the best, it's time to seal the deal. Sometimes it's difficult for parties to take that step. How do you successfully finalize the deal?

CLOSING THE DEAL

The following signs indicate that it is time to finalize:

- When the other party can no longer match you, the limit is reached.

- When the difference between what you and the other person want to achieve is minimum.
- Time is running out. Either accept the deal under these conditions or go home without a result.
- You don't have any more room to bargain. You can't make any more concessions. You've hit your bottom price.
- You've reached your objectives. Stop trying to get more, you're there. Close the deal.

The moment a negotiation enters its final phase, sometimes parties can become uneasy. Suddenly they become uncertain about the compromise on the table. One party might even decide to pull out. If the other party continues to be uncertain, the following can be applied.

Create the right environment

Show you appreciate their efforts to break deadlock. Then, summarize the mutual benefits that both parties will get from the deal. Indicate how much joint effort has been made. Confidently let them know that the deal will have a good outcome.

Give choices

Don't put the other party on the spot. If they are getting cold feet, don't try to force them to choose from only one option, if the deal doesn't go through. Propose several versions. Comfort them with their choices. Give them the feeling that they can still influence the outcome.

Act like you already agreed

Sometimes you can give the other party the final push by simply acting like you already agreed. You explain the compromise, confirm the terms of the agreement, and thank them for their cooperation and efforts. What also helps is if you start writing on a piece of paper the points that you both agree on: "we agreed on ..."

No longer ask if they agree to the compromise. Act as if you've already decided on that with each other, and that you are just summarizing the highlights on paper.

Having objections

Fear of risks and lingering doubts block the other party from getting to a compromise. Never ignore their objections, address them, and bend them slowly. The following techniques will help you:

Isolating objections

Pull out the biggest objection and future pace them. "If we just forget for a moment the term of the contract being five years, what would you think about the deal *then*?" By having the other party experience the rest of the agreement positively, you keep them focused on closing the deal. If necessary, make a tentative agreement and move past the snag that they are hung up about. Only when you iron that out, the entire agreement is final.

Bending

Don't try to change the objectives of the other party during the final stage. Go along with their objectives and emphasize the benefits you're both getting out of the deal. It is a significant investment on your part. It will certainly start to pay off after two years. But it's still a lot of money. Instead of ignoring his concern, it's better to recognize it and take it seriously. You cannot convince him anymore, he has to do that himself. And of course, point out what he's getting out of the deal.

THE BENEFIT OF MAKING A DEAL VERSUS THE DISADVANTAGE OF NO DEAL

Some people focus on avoiding risks while others see the benefits that can be achieved from taking them. The argument "this insurance prevents you from having to pay additional equity with declining foreign exchange rates" will appeal to a party who hates risks. However, with someone who's more concerned with possibilities, the remark will have little effect. He would prefer to hear: "this insurance allows you the possibility to speculate on price increases or decreases." By emphasizing both aspects you'll communicate to both types of people.

IMAGINE...

"Suppose we omit this wording. Would you sign the agreement then?" This way, you find out where the biggest hitch is. If the other party confirms your suggestion, you've implicitly got consent from him to go ahead and close the deal. If you get a negative reply, then he obviously has other objections you need to find out. Perhaps the next question will help.

WHAT DO I NEED TO DO TO GET YOU TO CLOSE TO THE DEAL?

Asking what you still need to do will help reveal the difficult issue the other party has. That's the best - and quickest way - to find out the status quo. You're not likely to hear a firm "no". At this stage of the game, the advantages outweigh the disadvantages, and their hesitations are slight. Now, the main question is: are you willing to concede to their final demands?

Remain critical to the end

With the end in sight, the other party might convince you to accept a compromise that is not beneficial to your interests and objectives. During this stage there are several risk involved.

When a negotiation has been a difficult process, both parties are relieved that a compromise is in view. The urge to get results often blinds both parties, and they sometimes forget to consider their objectives. In hindsight, you don't want your backers to think you compromised too easily. Especially when the negotiations are entering their final phase, the negotiator has to keep his wits. Don't give in too quickly. Take time to think about the final proposal. Suspend the meeting to consult with others. Compare the final deal with your initial proposal and objectives, consider your alternatives, the proxy that you had been given, and and discuss it with your backers.

Inform your backers

Sometimes selling the final deal to those whom you are working for requires a lot of energy and demands being creative. If you haven't kept them updated on the negotiations and sufficiently tempered their expectations from the beginning, it is going to be difficult selling the final deal.

When you are negotiating on behalf of a group, it's your responsibility to keep them in the loop about the developments throughout the negotiations. Regularly inform them of the status quo. Don't give them any unrealistic expectations on how they stand to gain from the talks. Let them know that not all their objectives can be met and that they should be prepared to make concessions. Also let them know that the other party is likely not to make concessions. Have them consider alternatives and allow them to anticipate modest results. This gives you more leeway during the talks, and allows you to manage the expectations of your backers.

When presenting the final deal, emphasize the results you achieved and the concrete objectives that have been met. If you have to inform them that they did not get everything they wanted, never do this at the beginning of your presentation. Start with one or two negotiating points that you've won, then with what wasn't achieved, and conclude with the overal success of the negotations. Also include the concessions made by the other party. Your backers will not only be satisfied with the substance of the deal, but they should also have a feeling that it was a fair deal, with give and take from both sides. Act excited about what you've accomplished, and never show your doubts about the final results. This jeopardizes your credibility, and gives the impression that you were not tough enough, and that they should have had another negotator.

Put the agreement in writing

When you end the negotiations write the agreement down. This prevents other things than what you had agreed on coming up later. It won't take much time, and it's worth it in the end.

DIRTY TRICK
CONTINUOUSLY PRESSURING

Getting a far-reaching proposal through is almost impossible. However, if the same proposal is continuously presented in different forms, again and again, over a long period of time, chances are that it will be accepted by the other party. At first it seemed odd, but after continous repetition, the proposal doesn't look that bad. The more often a person hears something, after a while it starts to sound normal. Whether it's good or bad news. First we get used to the idea that the price of houses increases every year. Then we get used to the idea that house prices decrease every year. A homeowner who's not influenced by the outside world yet, may still think he's going to get a high price when he sells his house. Unfortunately, he has to accept a lower price in a declining market. Only after some time, when he watches TV and reads the newspapers, he is confronted with the declining real estate market. He gets used to the fact that he must accept a lower price. His perception has changed, again.

Clever negotiators apply this principle gradually. During informal meetings procurement representatives say that business is not going well and profits are down. When a seller hears these messages regularly throughout the year, then he'll stop consider increasing the prices. This signal has the same effect as a psychological anchor. Each time the two will meet this anchor will be triggered again. Consequently the buyer will unconsciously not raise his prices. He might even be apt to lower them. By gradually applying the same idea, the buyer influences the seller to offer lower prices and his market perception justifies a price reduction.

Whether adding pressure qualifies as a dirty trick, also depends on the intention. Sometimes an unlikely proposal is presented by first offering it in extreme version. Over the course of time, the negotiator will offer milder versions that will cause less resistance. However, the resistance decreases by getting used to the idea. The final proposal won't seem so bad, in comparison to the initial one. But's it still bad. The other party has just been worn down. When companies reorganize, the management sometime apply this trick.

Because of high labor costs, a company in the Deep South has to move a portion of the workforce abroad. By transferring business activities to another country, the local community stands to lose many jobs. The management expects approximately 300 FTE's to disappear over the course of three years. However, the trade unions were informed that 450 FTE's will be lost within one year. The workers are angry. There is dismay and disbelief everywhere on the workfloor. The union threatens legal action and are calling for a general strike if management implements their plans. After several weeks, the board comes up with a new plan. This time "only" 375 FTE's will be phased out over a year and a half. Again, the unions are up in arms. However, it is also clear that a large number of layoffs is insurmountable within a short time. After six months, the managment negotiates with the trade unions and presents their final reorganization plan. Over a period of two years, 300 FTE's will disappear. Of course, the employees are disappointed but in comparison to the original plan, less jobs will be lost. From their perception, that's a better deal.

It's difficult to know if a dirty trick has been played on you. Because you do not know in advance whether someone started with an exaggerated or overstated idea, or if he honestly played it down over time. A sure sign that it's a dirty trick is when the other party comes for a second time with an even more outlandish proposal. When this happens, you should be seeing a red flag and hearing alarms go off. It's orchestrated. The best thing to do is to emphasize that you do not see anything different from the previous version. Inform them if they want to discuss something new, then they should come up with alternatives to their original proposal.

DIRTY TRICK
THE FAKE NEGOTIATION

The other party acts like it wants to negotiate. However, they say that other issues need more attention before the deal can be sealed. You will be asked to provide more information that will help them make their decision. But even after you have met all their requests, they still need additional information from you. You feel like they are not really negotiating: they are toying with you and waiting for a better deal to come along.

The other party doesn't give you the impression as if they want to close a deal. They are only acting, and appear to be interested. They are just asking for important information that you would not normally give away, except during negotiations. The other party might be acting as if they are negotiating with you, only to keep you from negotiating with other parties in the market. Because you're negotiating with them, you're not shopping around with other parties. This way you are no longer a threat to them. In a situation like this, how can you protect yourself?

Determine beforehand, during the preparation phase, which information you are strategically willing to share with the other party. If the other party needs additional important information, then you can always demand that the information you provide be kept secret. Inform them that the information can only be provided under the same legal construction as a due diligence process. If the other party is serious about the negotiations, then they should be willing to comply with your request.

Demand that the deal be finalized after the important requirement has been fulfilled and it meets the conditions or criteria of the other party.

If the whole process is starting to take too long, start looking for new parties to start negotiating with. Let the other party know that you are also talking with other parties.

DIRTY TRICK
LACK OF AUTHORIZATION

After a long strenuous negotiation it's finally time to sign the agreement. At the last moment, the other party suddenly tells you that they are not authorized to sign off on the deal. Their supervisor has to study the agreement first before the deal can be finalized.

The supervisor assures you there is no reason to worry: "In general, the concept looks good, however for the exception of a few items, my negotiator seems to have been too generous at times. So it looks like we have to renegotiate."

What now? You have already given all your information and made all your possible concessions. You've played all your cards.

In cases like these, the only cure is prevention. Ask at the start of the negotiation if your partner is authorized to sign.

"How much of proxy do you have?" If you think that is too confrontational, you might opt for a more subtle "I take it you are authorized to close the deal?" Or, "I am authorized to sign, I expect you are too?" Another one is "How far can we go with negotiations?"

However, if you are confronted with this trick while closing a deal, you can always fight fire with fire. Give yourself some bargaining leeway and say for example that you still have to discuss the results with your backers. Of course, it's always up to them to agree. Another option is to have someone else replace you for the next round of negotiations.

After long and intense negotiations in which concessions are swapped back and forth, a deal is finally ironed out. Then you get a telephone call from the other negotiator, "Sorry, unfortunately I can't get the deal approved." The head office won't sign off on the deal. There are two clauses that need to be adapted and your fees need to reduced by 10% before my guys will approve. Otherwise we do not have a deal."

This dirty trick is a variation of the "not enough authority." Here, too, it is important not to act hasty. Do not make any quick concessions. Determine whether the conditions are a problem. If you are willing to commit to their demands, then ask them for a concession. It's important to get something back.

Let the other party know that you do not approve. This is not a way to do business. Your offer was a final offer, regardless of who needs to authorize it. Ask if you can speak directly to the person in charge. If he is bluffing, the other party will be treading backwards. Stick to your original deal.

Putting on the pressure

There comes a time when you need to let the other party know you are not going to negotiate "until kingdom come." If you've reached the end of the your tether, then you should specify your time limit. Don't be too quick to let them know your time restrictions, because it could also be perceived as a deadline. When you let them know you have a deadline, you essentially hand over your bargaining power. However, when all the other tricks haven't worked, it's time to apply pressure. Applying pressure is a way of forcing a decision. At the same time, emphasize what the benefits of the deal will be for the other party, and point out what the disadvantages will be if they do not close the deal. Are they really worth the consequences of not accepting the deal? Let the other party draw their conclusions.

DIRTY TRICK
"SPLIT THE DIFFERENCE?"

Negotiations are stranded. Each party has asked the other one for concessions. During the talks, you've given all the concessions you are willing to make and you have reached your limit. The same applies to the other party. However, now the other party comes up with a plan: "Let's split the difference and close the deal."

At first, this proposal seems perfectly reasonable. After all you've both been negotiating for quite some time and the end is so close. However, beware. It can also be a quick way to make you give away another concession. Especially after all the concessions you've already done. Decide first, if, on the whole, everything is divided evenly.

Don't accept the proposal. Let the other party know that you have reached your limits. Ask the other party to list the concessions that they have done during the negotiations. Ask them to make a concession to finalize the deal. Apparently they still have some bargaining room if they are willing to "split the difference." Now, the ball is in their court. Prolong the deadlock and have them come up with an offer that will be more beneficial to you.

DIRTY TRICK
THE NIBBLE

The nibble trick is usually used at the end of the negotiation. You are about to successfully conclude negotiations, and just as you want to finalize the talks the other party confronts you with just one, last little requirement. It is often very small, but still. After all, you don't want the negotiations to fail on account of this minor request. The other party is aware of this, and they are testing you out. Let them know that you do not appreciate being surprised by a new concession this late in the game. Don't immediately make the concession. First ask them for something in return.

DIFFERENT INTERPRETATION

A housing cooperation is in the midst of a major change program. It's overhauling its strategy and structure that will change its business processes and IT systems. A renowned international consulting agency has been hired for the process. The discussions about the approach and negotiations for the tender went smoothly. A few weeks after the implementation of the project starts, the housing cooperation is getting worried. The way the consulting agency is implementing the change is not what the board of directors of the housing cooperation had anticipated. The CFO complains, "The interviews with our employees is taking too long." He adds, " and our employees feel uneasy with all those consultants running around. Moreover, they are very young. I hope that the consultants who will be leading the IT workshop will not be that young. Not once have I seen a senior partner come by yet. Who's running this show?" He continues, "I had expected at least a senior partner to be chairing the meetings with management. I don't think that young woman who presides over our meetings is very convincing. She can't unit the MT." "You're right," the chairman responds. I want an explanation from the partner."

Some time later, the steering committee meets and the partner from the consulting agency says he understands the housing cooperation's concerns but also points out the terms of the agreement: "It's absolutely necessary that the interviews be conducted. It is the basis of our reorganization plans for your business. We're not here for a quick win. We want to ensure that there is long term struc-

tural continuity and flexibility implemented in the functionality of your business processeses and automation system. They are our main priority for the long term. Your documentation hasn't been updated in a long time which made identifying and analyzing take much longer. Unfortunately, we could not anticipate that it take so long. I am leading the process, and I will instruct the consultants. No strategic decisions are made without my approval. Moreover, I oversee all documentation, and I am ultimately responsible."

The board of the housing cooperation is not satisfied with the partner's explanation. The chairman says irritatedly, "Thanks for your explanation, but we don't consider interviews to be in-depth business analysis. However, that is not our main issue. Our problem is your leadership. We expected 'on the work-floor' visiblity from you. We assumed that you would chair plenary meetings with our employees, and that you would preside over the meetings with our board during this project. Your presence and advice have an enormous impact. The junior consultants lack experience."

The partner responds, "I understand your concerns but I do not agree with you." He continues, "Our people have extensive experience with similar projects and organizations. If you want me to have a leading role in the operational management of the project, that is possible, but we did not include that in the contract. That would mean that I would have to invest more time and I would have to declare more hours for the project."

By now, the board members are really irritated. "Operational leaders?" stammers the chairman of the board. "That's crazy! What's the difference between being a project leader and responsible for the final project?"

"I guess we have a difference of interpretation," responds the partner. "Let's see how we can reach a solution that suits both of us. I'm willing to preside over your plenary sessions and meetings. That means more time on my part. For that, I won't charge the full amount. I'm making you a big offer."

At this point, the board of directors have gotten really upset. Not only because of the extra costs, but because they feel like they have been cheated. Continuing with junior consultants will only undermine the project's success. So, should they then accept the partner's proposal?

Of course, the board of directors should have been more specific when they drafted the agreement. But even when agreements are drafted by lawyers, it is not unusual for differences of interpretation to occur when deals and projects are implemented. Most of the time there is no ill intent, but sometimes there can be. How can you prevent this situation?

It is always wise to focus on how the contract will be implemented right from the start of a project. Immediately let the other party know when your expectations are not being met. In the beginning it is difficult for the other party to start making demands because the process is still in the early phase. It is easier for your to call off the deal because you still haven't invested much time and money in the project. By giving the other party a clear signal from the beginning, you let them know you are on top of things and willing to call off the deal if they start to go off course.

In advance, you can decide with the other party how you

want to deal with differences in interpretation and address other disputes. This can be done by appointing an independent party to resolve differences. If this has not been done beforehand, you can also do one of the following.

You have to realize that the other party wants to improve its results for the betterment of the business relationship. Use this notion to put pressure on the existing relationship. "If this is the way we are going to do business, then we will stop right now. Any incurred costs will be charged immediately." The other party will be alarmed because they don't want to stop and lose money. If you cannot frighten them with this kind of gesture or you are too dependent on them, you can always threaten them with the remark "In the future we won't be doing any business with you. *And* we will inform others of how you do business."

Then, of course, there is always a nicer and more positive approach. Let them know that you would like to do business with them in the future, but that it largely depends on how the project works out. You can always add, if they do this job really well, that you will recommend them highly to others. That's sure to work.